Hamlyn Colour Guides
Climbing
Plants

Hamlyn Colour Guides
Climbing Plants

by Jan Tykač

Illustrated by
František Severa

Hamlyn

Translated by Dana Hábová
Graphic design by Miloš Lang
Designed and produced for Hamlyn Publishing
A division of The Hamlyn
Publishing Group Limited
Bridge House, London Road, Twickenham,
Middlesex, England

ISBN 0 600 30 570 8
Printed in Czechoslovakia
3/15/11/51-01

CONTENTS

CHARACTERISTICS OF CLIMBING PLANTS

Climbing plants are rooted in the ground and form long, usually weak, thinly branched and highly flexible herbaceous or woody stems. They can be naturally ascending or creeping at first, but later need support, around which to twine or cling to, to reach a favourable position in the light. In the wild the support is provided by surrounding plants, tree trunks, rocks or boulders, in gardens and sun rooms climbers twine around, cling to or lean against metal or wooden constructions. If no support is available, climbing plants tend to creep along the ground or overhang other plants.

There are more than 2,000 species of climbing plants, but relatively few of them are found wild in Britain and Europe. However, these do include some species of clematis, honeysuckle, ivy and climbing rose. Some species have been introduced and have become naturalized. Many climbing plants occur in the wild in the tropical rain forests of Africa, South America and on the Pacific islands. Other species are found in light woodlands, on the edges of woods and on scrub-covered slopes in the subtropical regions of south-eastern Asia, North America, or around the Mediterranean Sea.

Climbers can be divided into several groups, based on their mode of support. The most common are plants with twining stems. The apex of the stem grows upward and seeks a solid object by making circular movements. As soon as it touches a support, it starts to twine around it. Most twine in an anticlockwise direction, e.g. Dutchman's pipe (*Aristolochia*), celastrus, bindweed (*Convolvulus*), bean (*Phaseolus*) and wisteria. Those species twining in a clockwise direction comprise fallopia, hop (*Humulus*) and honeysuckle (*Lonicera*). Some, like convolvulus, are extremely active. This can wind its stem around a support once in two hours. Other species twine more slowly but develop considerable strength: for instance the stems of wisterias can strangle a young tree or crush a gutter pipe.

Many tropical climbing plants form special thin, flexible, sometimes branched tendrils with sensitive tips. When one of these tips touches a support, it starts to wind around it. Stem tendrils are produced by Virginia Creeper and Boston Ivy (*Parthenocissus*), passion flower (*Passiflora*), Cup-and-saucer Plant (*Cobaea*), gourd (*Cucurbita*) and peas (*Lathyrus*) have leaf tendrils. Some ivies form tendrils with terminal discs exuding a mucous, quickly solidifying secretion enabling them to cling to smooth surfaces. *Gloriosa* is equipped with hooks on the tips of leaves and uses them to hold to a support. Some climbers, like clematis and nasturtium (*Tropaeolum*), also use long twining petioles or even flower stalks for the same purpose.

Other species of climbing plants carry special adhesive adventitious roots, especially on young shoots. They are called self-clinging plants and include e.g. trumpet creeper (*Campsis*), spindle (*Euonymus*), *Ficus pumila,* ivy, hydrangea.

Some climbers make use of aerial roots growing on the stems. When these roots reach the ground, they get established in the soil and help to feed the plant. Some house plants like philodendrons, monsteras and other plants from tropical rain forests behave in this manner.

Other species are usually called scramblers: their long shoots either lean against a support or scramble over a shrub, rock or a suitable construction. Many, like climbing roses, brambles, Winter Jasmine or bougainvilleas, use thorns or short lateral twigs to help them cling.

This book also includes a number of plants that are not true climbers but possess a similar habit of growth. They are not twining and they lack adhesive organs. They have to be tied to a support or allowed to creep or hang down like members of the *Aeschynanthus* and the *Columnea* genera.

USES OF CLIMBING PLANTS

Few plants offer such a wide scale use as climbing, creeping and trailing plants. They can be planted and grown in the garden or in a sun room or conservatory. They include undemanding plants suitable for beginners, and plants with more taxing requirements that only an experienced grower can cope with. By the graceful elegance of their blossoms, foliage and fruits, or by the compact green screen created by their stems, they give a special soothing touch to homes and gardens. When decorating a house or garden with climbers, one can give free rein to one's imagination, and exploit all their qualities in attractive displays. They can be used as solitary plants, green 'cascades' over a wall, screens, ground cover, or even as a dominating feature in a flower arrangement situated in a large container.

Even the smallest garden can have its climbers, because, on the whole, they need little space. Various garden constructions such as porches, arbours, dividing walls and fences can be improved by climbing plants, and they can be used to mask unsightly walls, sheds and other constructions. Their requirements as to protection and maintenance are generally minimal.

PLANTS ON WALLS

Walls can be decorated with plants in two ways: the stems are either allowed to hang down, or they are trained up the wall. Most interior walls have to be equipped with a suitable and inconspicuous support. A simple and tasteful solution can consist of erecting a wooden or plastic trellis, or stretching plastic-covered, straining wires from a point behind the base of the plant in a fan. The wire must not touch the wall otherwise the stems will not be able to hold on.

If the plant is to cover a large surface, it needs a large container so the root system can develop. The most common containers are made of terra cotta, ceramic or plastic. The container is placed on the floor, filled with compost and the climber is planted directly or is plunged in a pot. The wall should never entirely disappear beneath the greenery; the climbers should only brighten it.

Hanging plants are situated in a room to display their trailing stems. An effective means of display is to place a pot or bowl on a solid glass plate shelf fixed on the wall. The pot can be put in an attractive pot holder to prevent spoiling the wall or the shelf when the plant is watered.

These hanging plants produce a beautiful effect when hung in a suspended pot holder provided it will not be in the way and the light is adequate.

Traditional pots and window boxes are not the only containers available. The plants look attractive in hanging baskets or coconut shells. The upper part of the shell is cut off, the flesh scooped out,

Hydroponic cultivation of climbing plants

holes are drilled on the sides and bast or coconut fibre is pulled through them to hang the plant. Two to three plants will fit in one shell. Coconut shells and hanging baskets are particularly suitable for ceropegia, peperomia, cissus, columnea, scindapsus and others.

The root balls dry out fast in all hanging containers, and the plants have to be watered regularly. The best method is to let the pot or container soak up moisture by immersing it in water. It is saturated when air bubbles no longer rise up. Excessive water is allowed to drain and the plant is returned to its place. If this method cannot be used, watering must be done with care or choose a container with a built-in drip tray. Check the plants from time to time in case excessive water accummulates to cause waterlogging. The other extreme — the compost drying out completely — must also be avoided.

Beside the traditional way of cultivating plants in compost, most climbing house plants can be grown hydroponically. However, detailed advice on hydroponics is beyond the scope of this book.

DIVIDING WALLS

Modern homes often feature dividing walls or partitions. They can be made of wood or metal, brick or plastic moulded blocks, stands and shelves. Young plants can be tied to a decorative trellis to form an attractive screen. Later, when they have become established, they will support themselves. A highly ornamental partition should be complemented with small-leaved, non-flowering plants, while a simple dividing wall can be draped with more flamboyant and larger-leaved species. Plants of a trailing habit are better suited for a dividing wall composed of shelves. All containers must be absolutely waterproof to prevent unnecessary damage caused by watering.

MOSS STICKS AND OTHER SUPPORTS

Florists sometimes offer climbing plants trained to sticks covered with moss peat. The plants are usually ivies, monsteras, philodendrons and scindapsus. To form handsome green columns, the plants need a stick on which the moss is kept moist by frequent spraying with water. Other supports for young climbers consist of ladder-like devices of wood or plastic, or three sticks inserted along the edge of a pot. The plants twine around these supports or are tied into place.

PLANTS IN TROPICAL WINDOWS AND VITRINES

More demanding species of climbing, creeping and hanging plants, particularly those occurring in the wild in tropical rain forests, require high atmospheric humidity. This can only be provided in a closed space in temperate regions, either in a heated conservatory or in a flower window or vitrine. The taxing requirements of these plants cannot be met without an efficient heating system and good light. Their eventual size should always be taken into account when the plants are arranged to form a balanced display. A thoughtfully composed flower window will be a stunning feature in any room.

The tropical window is a sort of permanent greenhouse in a room, with one side formed by the window. It must be situated in a position from which the plants can be viewed best. The best orientation is 'facing the north-west or north-east. Dimensions and depth are adapted to the existing window. Care of plants in the tropical window consists of maintaining temperature and humidity, and adequate ventilation and regular feeding. Treatment is similar to that given to plants standing freely indoors.

To provide easy access to the plants, the glass pane facing the room has to slide freely or be removable. The plants are usually set out in a metal or ceramic container filled with peat, gravel, or other suitable material. This material depends to some extent on the choice of plants. The base container should be at least 25 cm (10 in) wide and 15 cm (6 in) deep. The heating of the tropical window should be independent of the heating system of the flat or house. The usual

Planted tropical window
with lateral sliding panes

source of heat is a heating cable with a thermostat. Independent heating facilitates thermal regulation over 24 hours: the night temperature should be lower by several degrees than the day temperature. The central-heating system in the house is often turned off during the day and the maximum heat is felt during the evening. A deeper window densely planted will need additional light provided by fluorescent tubes to extend the day length in winter.

The tropical window can accommodate a large number of heat-loving plants. Smaller plants of hanging or climbing habit can be placed on a piece of branch wood or suspended in space. Creeping plants are set out by the base of a piece of branch wood where they spread and form a thick ground cover. Climbing plants are also situated against a branch which they can cling to.

A vitrine can be used for the same purpose as the tropical window. Unlike the permanently established window, the vitrine is mobile or portable. It can be like a small greenhouse on wheels which can be opened out to display the plants or like a terrarium which can be obtained in a range of shapes and sizes. The technical equipment is the same as in the window.

11

CLIMBING PLANTS FOR BALCONIES AND PATIOS

Balcony and window boxes are ideal for petunias and trailing pelargoniums. Trailing fuchsias, asparagus ferns and ivy will flourish in tubs or hanging baskets in shady spots. Loggia walls can be covered from spring to autumn with runner beans, sweet peas, morning glory and other climbing annuals.

CLIMBING PLANTS IN THE GARDEN

Climbing plants serve many purposes in gardens. They are excellent subjects for covering garage walls, sheds, fences and any unsightly objects; they festoon them with their greenery, mask their unsightly appearance and generally brighten them up. The colour of leaves or flowers of the chosen species or cultivar must be in contrast with the shade of the wall. Red roses look superb against a white-washed wall, while yellow or white roses go better with a brick wall.

Only self-clinging plants can hold onto a rough-surfaced wall; others have to be given a support. Wooden or plastic trellis or plastic-covered wire stretched between wire eyes are the most efficient methods. The support must be situated at least 5 cm (2 in) from the wall. For a fast-growing cover it is best to choose vigorous-growing climbing species, such as Russian Vine, honeysuckle, clematis species. Some annuals such as Cup-and-saucer Plant, sweet peas, runner beans, nasturtium or a gourd give a good quick cover but unfortunately annuals flower briefly and die down in autumn.

A house covered by climbing plants is a welcome sight in a drab street. The plants create a sort of air cushion with a favourable microclimate around the house, cutting down the heat loss, while the dense foliage protects the walls from cold winds.

It is a mistake to believe that climbing plants damage brickwork. Some people think that a wall covered by greenery will become damp. This is not true, because the shingle-like arrangement of leaves prevents the rain from affecting the walls. The water drips from one leaf to another, eventually to the ground. As for any worry that foundations will be damaged by damp and roots, it has been found that the roots of woody plants work like pumps and siphon away all moisture, tending to dry out the foundations. It is also believed that climbing plants provide habitats for unpleasant insects. This cannot be entirely refuted, but the same can be said about any plant anywhere in the garden. However, these insects serve as food for songbirds which find climbing plants ideal for nesting.

Fences made of wire netting, concrete, bricks or even wood often look unattractive. Metal fences can look severe, but their appearance can be softened and improved by climbing plants. A densely-covered fence will form a clear boundary around the garden and so create a cosy and intimate atmosphere. The fence, however, has to be stable enough to carry the weight of the plants. It is advisable to choose species reaching to 2 to 3 m (6 to 10 ft) in height, needing little room and having modest soil requirements. Best suited are various species of clematis, honeysuckle and Russian Vine.

The natural grace of akebias, actinidias, aristolochias and celastruses can be displayed against walls or over pillars or posts of garden gates. If the posts are very thick, a wooden or metal stick has to be fastened to them for the plants to twine around or cling to. A strung wire serves the same purpose. The posts can be connected on top by horizontal poles to form a simple pergola over which a variety of plants can be trained. Two plants either of the same species or different can be set out against each upright construction.

A garden wall may sometimes feature a nicely-shaped, decorative trellis. This can be festooned with climbers, but, for the best effect, never entirely covered.

A dead or living tree trunk also makes good support for climbing plants. The trunk of a large oak, beech or acacia covered in ivy looks more lush than bare wood. In years to come the plants will climb up to the crown without damaging the tree, providing it is healthy. Very attractive is a living curtain made of climbers: a long chain or strong wire is suspended from a bough and a vigorous-growing climber is planted underneath. It will have to be tied in place at first, but later it will use the support to climb up to the treetop.

Some small trailing plants — evergreen euonymus, ivies, periwinkles — can be planted in crevices between stones in a dry wall. Winter Jasmine, Japanese Honeysuckle, some large-flowered clematis could be successfully planted on the top. Some species like periwinkle, ivy and evergreen euonymus are popular as ground cover plants, because they are capable of forming a continuous green carpet in a short time. In shady places they can be a substitute for grass. Clematis species and honeysuckle can be planted on steep slopes where they are allowed to grow without support and cover the whole area.

PERGOLAS

A pergola plays a specific part in the garden and therefore deserves some extra attention. It is an important visual element in dividing up the garden and so making it more intimate. It can link up the various parts of the garden with the house. Its shady seclusion is much appreciated on hot sunny summer days.

A classic pergola consists of two rows of vertical columns connected on top by horizontal transverse poles which form a ceiling. The height should be 2.2 to 2.5 m (7 to 8 ft); if it is any lower the trailing shoots tend to get in the way of people sitting or walking underneath. The corridor between the two rows of columns ideally should be 3 m (10 ft) wide. A narrow passage soon becomes difficult to walk through or turns into a dark tunnel. The construction must be strong to resist gusts of wind and to bear the weight of the plants. The building materials should be chosen to blend in with the character of the house. Wooden pergolas made of rustic poles or treated wooden posts are the most common today, although brick pillars can look most attractive. All the parts must fit together well to ensure the joints are waterproof. Wood should be given a protective coating of cuprinol or other treatment not toxic to plants, which is renovated regularly. The most natural colours are shades of brown, although light colour hues, white or cream, are more cheerful. A treatment enhancing the natural texture of the wood is the most effective.

Climbing plants are set at the foot of each column. If the columns are very thick, a stick or lengths of plastic-coated wire have to be provided for the plants to climb on in the early stages of growth.

When selecting plants for a pergola, their requirements as to sunshine or shade have to be taken in to consideration. Climbers that look attractive draped over a pergola include akebias, aristolochias, trumpet creepers, Russian Vine, wisterias, honeysuckles and some clematis species. Annuals (except perhaps gourds) are usually too low growing for this purpose although morning glory can be stunning given a good position.

SYSTEMATIC NOTE

The texts accompanying the illustrations in many cases introduce varieties in addition to original species. Varieties are naturally occurring, botanical subdivisions of a species unlike cultivars which have been derived by breeding. These latter differ from the original species in various ways, usually larger flowers or improved colour range, which they retain when propagated vegetatively by cuttings or layers, but not from seed.

COLOUR ILLUSTRATIONS

Indian Mallow
Abutilon megapotamicum   Malvaceae

Almost 100 species of *Abutilon* are found predominantly in subtropical South America.

The Brazilian species *Abutilon megapotamicum,* formerly referred to as *A. vexillarium,* is cultivated as an ornamental woody plant. It is a deciduous shrub reaching a height of about 1 m (3 ft) with thin, pendent branches. It can be grown successfully outdoors in mild areas and should be planted by a south- or west-facing wall for best effect.

It can be grown as an indoor plant in colder regions and has no special requirements as regards temperature, providing it is above freezing. It needs plenty of light in winter and moderate watering at an optimum temperature of 6 to 8 °C (43 to 46 °F). However, if you want the plants to flower in winter, a temperature of 12 to 14 °C (53 to 57 °F) must be assured to prevent leaf fall. It needs a sunny position and from mid-May to September it can be stood out on a balcony, terrace or patio, or the plant can be inserted in the ground in a sheltered position in the garden.

When in full growth, pot-grown specimens require regular watering and an application of liquid fertilizer every two weeks. In spring long shoots are cut back by half and older specimens should be transplanted into larger pots with a rich soil-based compost.

For indoor cultivation, it is better to grow new plants every year. Softwood cuttings without flower buds, about 8 cm (3 in) long, are taken in March or August. If kept in a propagating frame at 20 to 22 °C (68 to 71 °F) they should take root within three weeks. Abutilon can also be propagated from seeds sown in March; the seedlings usually take two years to start flowering.

Abutilon megapotamicum (1) is a rewarding indoor plant. It flowers best in spring and summer. The flowers and leaves persist throughout winter if sufficient light and adequate temperature are provided. Most people enjoy the tree-like shape displaying the elegant pendent branches. The stem is about 1 m (3 ft) tall. The luxuriantly growing *A. pictum* 'Thompsonii' is sometimes used as rootstock to produce larger plants which, like most abutilons, will need staking.

Abutilon megapotamicum 'Variegatum' (2) has leaves marbled with yellow. The pattern is caused by a virus and can be transferred by grafting to green-leaved plants.

2

1

Chinese Gooseberry
Actinidia chinensis

Actinidiaceae

Actinidias are climbing deciduous plants. Twenty-five species have been discovered so far, all in south-eastern and eastern Asia.

Actinidia chinensis is not widely grown. It is a rather demanding twining plant native to eastern Asia. In Britain and Europe it can be most successfully cultivated in areas where vines grow well as it needs similar conditions. Its fruits are multi-seeded berries rich in vitamins, and breeders, mostly in New Zealand, have produced cultivars yielding larger fruits suitable for less favourable climates.

Another occasionally grown species is *Actinidia arguta,* indigenous to Japan, China and Korea. This twining shrub may reach a height of 6 m (20 ft) under favourable conditions. The fruits are yellow-green to brownish-green, sweet-tasting berries, about 2.5 cm (1 in) long. *A. kolomikta* originates from the same area. Although it is frost-hardy, it rarely surpasses the height of 6 m (20 ft). The fruits are blue-black and sweet, but are not often produced.

Actinidias do best in partial shade and in humus- and nutrient-rich soil with plenty of moisture. Species of actinidia are propagated from seeds sown under glass or by hardwood cuttings taken in November. Cultivars are grafted on *A. kolomikta* rootstocks in March or April.

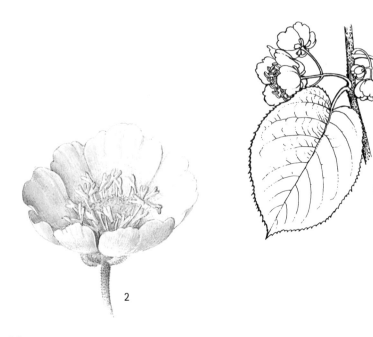

2

3

Actinidia chinensis (1) is native to China and Taiwan. It can reach up to 8 m (26 ft) in height under favourable conditions. Its 5-cm (2-in) long fruits resemble gooseberries and are imported to Europe under the name of Kiwi fruits. In the garden it should be planted against a wall, or trained to cover a pergola or column which it uses for support. It can also climb up older trees or bushy shrubs, or like raspberries along wines. This species has creamy, sweet-scented blossoms (2).

Actinidias are dioecious, with fruits developing only from the flowers of female plants. A male plant (3) has to be nearby to serve as a pollinator. However, a branch with male blossoms grafted in the crown of a female plant will do.

Lipstick Plant
Aeschynanthus radicans
Gesneriaceae

Over 60 species of the genus *Aeschynanthus* grow predominantly in south-eastern Asia. They are mostly evergreen, epiphytic sub-shrubs of trailing habit. They differ from the related genus *Columnea* in having smooth, hairless leaves. The flowers are arranged in clusters and the fruits elongated.

    Aeschynanthus radicans is a dependable, flowering, trailing plant which is best displayed on a high shelf, in a hanging basket or in a closed window or a glass vitrine. It produces long shoots soon masking the pot. *A. radicans* is still occasionally referred to as *Trichosporum lobbianum*. *A. radicans* flourishes at a temperature of 20 to 25 °C (68 to 77 °F) and requires high atmospheric humidity. In winter the temperature should never drop below 18 °C (64 °F). The plants are prone to sunscorch, and therefore prefer a window with an easterly or westerly aspect where the direct rays of the sun cannot harm the foliage.

    Like other species of this genus, *Aeschynanthus radicans* requires regular watering when in full growth and an application of liquid fertilizer every two weeks. Throughout the winter the plants are left to rest and watered very sparingly to allow them to start forming flower buds.

    Older specimens are usually repotted once in two years, preferably in spring, into shallow bowls or baskets filled with peat-based, well-drained compost.

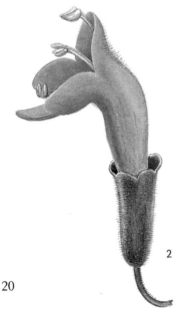

2

Aeschynanthus radicans (1) comes from the mountain forests of Java. The tubular flowers are up to 6 cm (2¼ in) long and appear mainly from June to September. Their effect is stunning if associated with a piece of branch wood.

    The flower tube emerges from the sepals (2) which remain decorative even after flowering has finished. Under favourable conditions the flowers last throughout summer when the plants do not require much attention. After flowering, an elongated fruit containing seeds with feathery appendages may be formed. Propagation is by softwood or stem cuttings with two pairs of leaves.

1

The cuttings are inserted by three or five
pieces into 8-cm (3-in) pots. They take
root readily in a propagation frame with
bottom heat kept at a temperature of
22 to 25 °C (71 to 77 °F).

Aeschynanthus speciosus

Gesneriaceae

Aeschynanthus speciosus, also known as *Trichosporum splendens,* is native to the forests of Indonesia. The stems grow erect at first and later become pendent and woody at the base. The leaves are up to 10 cm (4 in) long. *A. speciosus* needs more warmth and humidity than *A. radicans.*

Aeschynanthus boscheanus is found in Java and Sumatra. The leaves are reddish-brown, only 2.5 cm (1 in) long. The sepals are brownish-red, the flower red with a yellow pattern. Flowering lasts from June to August. *A. marmoratus* grows in Burma, Thailand and Indonesia. It has elongated, lanceolate leaves up to 10 cm (4 in) long, pale green with a dark marbled pattern. The underside is reddish-purple. The flowers are only 2.5 cm (1 in) long, green and spotted with brown. Under favourable conditions the flowering carries on throughout the year.

Aeschynanthus parasiticus comes from Assam. It is a relatively hardy species with large leaves and orange, dark-patterned flowers, up to 5 cm (2 in) long and have protruding stamens.

Aeschynanthus × *splendidus* is a hybrid of *A. parasiticus* and *A. speciosus.* It has large, elongated, lanceolate leaves and scarlet flowers appearing from June to September.

A. tricolor is widespread in Borneo. The pendent shoots bear tiny, ovate, green leaves with a reddish flush. The flowering takes place mainly in June and July. The blossoms are clustered in threes or fives and have reddish sepals and yellow petals with scarlet streaking.

2

Aeschynanthus speciosus (1) bears clusters of 8-cm (3-in) long flowers at the tips of pendent stems. In indoor cultivation the flowering period lasts from June to September, but further flowering can be assured by providing favourable conditions. The fruits are elongated berries.

Aeschynanthus speciosus is suitable only for short-term cultivation indoors as a potted plant (2). It does better in a window vitrine where a temperature of at least 22 °C (71 °F) and high humidity are maintained. The plants do not tolerate winter temperatures below 15 °C (59 °F). Requirements as to light, watering and feeding are the same as for *A. radicans.* There is no distinct rest period in winter. Propagation is by cuttings.

1

23

The genus *Akebia* comprises only two species. Their native area is in eastern Asia. They are twining, vigorous woody plants with fine, alternate leaves shed late in the year.

Akebia quinata is usually grown in gardens where this undemanding twiner can create a pleasant shady spot. The plants are particularly effective in covering fences, walls or pergolas. The climbing habit can be used to cover the trunks of old trees, columns or other vertical constructions in the garden.

Akebias thrive in a warm site sheltered from cold winds, in well-drained soil. They tolerate both full sun and semi-shade. They are hardy enough to survive most winters.

Young plants should at first be tied to a stick or strong wire; later on they will use this support without being tied. Older shrubs often become bare in the lower parts; this is prevented by cutting back some shoots close to the main stem to promote new growths.

Propagation is usually by vegetative means. Layering is the simplest method. Some plants grow so many root suckers that these can become a nuisance. Akebias can also be raised from half-ripe cuttings taken in summer, from root cuttings, of from seed.

2

3

Akebia quinata (1) originates in China, Japan and Korea. It reaches a height of around 10 m (33 ft) and forms a thick tangle of thin, twining stems requiring support.

The delicately scented blossoms, about 2.5 cm (1 in) across, open in April and May, but they tend to be hidden by the dense cover of foliage. The female flowers (2) are larger than the male ones (3), but both occur in the same inflorescence.

In their native habitat and after a hot summer akebias produce fleshy, 5- to 10-cm (2-to 4-in) long, brown-purplish fruits covered with a bluish bloom, somewhat resembling cucumbers in shape. They open after ripening and reveal black seeds in gelatinous arils (4).

4

1

Allamanda cathartica   Apocynaceae

There are only 12 classified species of the genus *Allamanda*. They are mostly climbing woody plants with evergreen foliage, all found in tropical South America.

Allamanda cathartica is the most commonly grown species in Europe. It grows best in a greenhouse or a closed glass vitrine kept at an optimum temperature of 18 to 20 °C (64 to 68 °F). It requires plenty of light but has to be protected from full sun. The recommended winter temperature is 12 to 15 °C (53 to 59 °F).

From April to October allamanda is regularly watered and at the time of full growth it should be fed with a balanced liquid fertilizer once a fortnight. Watering is reduced towards the end of autumn and during winter according to the decreasing amount of light. Younger plants are repotted annually, the older ones just once every few years, in a standard soil-based potting compost. Old branches are cut back in February, before new growth starts, preferably to above the second whorl of leaves from the ground.

It is propagated from softwood cuttings with two to three whorls of leaves. They take root best in March in a propagating frame kept at a temperature of 20 to 22 °C (68 to 71 °F), inserted into 6-cm (2¼-in) pots. The plants should be supported with sticks in the pots from the very beginning. In five to six weeks young plants are potted into 10-cm (4-in) pots and after another six weeks the tips are pinched out to encourage branching. One-year-old plants can bear flowers. Growth regulating chemicals are used by growers to produce compact potted plants.

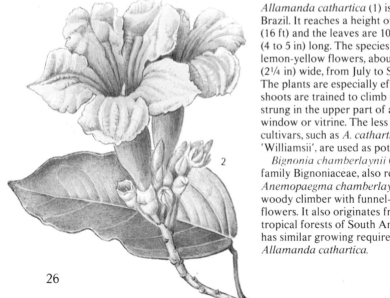

Allamanda cathartica (1) is native to Brazil. It reaches a height of up to 5 m (16 ft) and the leaves are 10 to 13 cm (4 to 5 in) long. The species produces lemon-yellow flowers, about 6 cm (2¼ in) wide, from July to September. The plants are especially effective if their shoots are trained to climb up wires strung in the upper part of a flower window or vitrine. The less vigorous cultivars, such as *A. cathartica* 'Williamsii', are used as potted plants.

Bignonia chamberlaynii (2) of the family Bignoniaceae, also referred to as *Anemopaegma chamberlaynii*, is another woody climber with funnel-shaped flowers. It also originates from the tropical forests of South America and has similar growing requirements to *Allamanda cathartica*.

1

27

Ampelopsis brevipedunculata

Vitaceae

Some 20 species of this genus are found predominantly in eastern Asia and North America. They are climbing shrubs with twining stems and tendrils.

Ampelopsis brevipedunculata is rarely grown as a house plant. In its natural habitat in eastern China it reaches a height of 6 to 10 cm (20 to 33 ft).

It can be grown in unheated greenhouses or conservatories, either in a soil border or in a large container. It can be trained up a trellis or tied to training wires.

In the growing period *Ampelopsis* requires ample watering and an application of balanced fertilizer once a fortnight. Plenty of light and fresh air are vital. It sheds leaves in winter and should be kept at a temperature of about 2 °C (35 °F). Watering should be kept to a minimum. In March the plant is cut back some 10 cm (4 in) above the soil level, transplanted, if necessary, into soil-based compost and watered more often. In a moderately warm and light situation it soon sprouts leaves.

Propagation by cuttings is usually carried out in August. Several softwood cuttings are placed in pot filled with a gritty compost. They root readily if kept in a warm place — a temperature of about 20 °C (68 °F) is ideal.

Ampelopsis brevipedunculata (1) has deciduous, lobed leaves, up to 13 cm (5 in) long, varying in shape. It supports itself by means of tendrils. It produces insignificant flowers during July and August. After a hot summer these flowers are followed by pea-sized fruits, which are greenish-brown and later turn blue-purple. The cultivar *A. brevipedunculata* 'Elegans' is much less vigorous and has white-spotted leaves with a pinkish sheen in the juvenile state. The mottled leaves turn greenish if planted in deep shade.

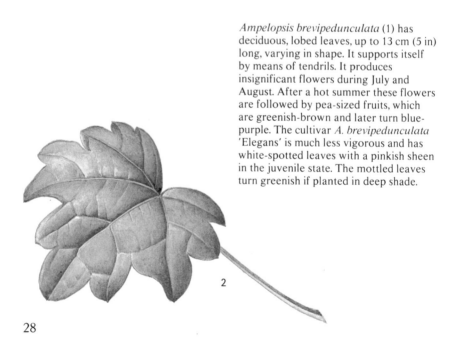

Ampelopsis japonica (2) is native to
Japan and northern China. In mild areas
this grows well if planted against a sunny
wall. This plant is also referred to as
A. serjaniifolia and *Vitis serjaniifolia.*

Flamingo Plant
Anthurium scandens   Araceae

Almost 500 species of this genus are found in tropical rain forests of South America. Most of them are erect perennials with evergreen, leathery leaves and showy flowers.

Anthurium scandens, one of the climbing species, is rarely grown as an indoor plant. The thin stem is almost all covered with adventitious roots. The leaves are up to 13 cm (5 in) long and vary greatly in shape.

This fast-growing species thrives at a temperature of approximately 22 °C (71 °F), in a humid atmosphere and protected from direct sun. It requires ample and regular watering from February to October. In December and January, it undergoes a four- to six-week period of rest when watering must be reduced and the temperature decreased to 15 to 17 °C (59 to 62 °F).

Propagating is by stem cuttings placed in a propagating frame with bottom heat where they take root and form new shoots at a temperature of 25 to 30 °C (77 to 86 °F). Seeds can be sown in a mixture of peat and sand, preferably in March. Seedlings and young plants are cultivated at a temperature of about 22 °C (71 °F). They grow erect during the early stages of their development but later have to be tied to a support or grown in hanging baskets. If necessary, they are transplanted in spring into a peat-based compost. These plants do not tolerate lime so should be watered with rain water.

3

Anthurium scandens (1) forms climbing stems which tend to trail unless a support is provided. They are very effective growing in a hanging container in a flower window or vitrine facing east or north-east, where high humidity can be maintained. The plant has shallow roots and nutrients have to be supplied by applying a weak solution of balanced liquid fertilizer every two weeks.

The cylindrical inflorescence (2) is formed by a 5-cm (2-in) long spadix, and the fruits are pea-sized berries containing seeds (3). In the cultivar 'Violaceum' the berries have a violet flush.

1

2

Dutchman's Pipe
Aristolochia elegans   Aristolochiaceae

The genus *Aristolochia* comprises over 300 species found mainly in the tropics and subtropics of America, Africa and Asia. Only a small number of species originate in the temperate zone of Europe and North America.

Aristolochia elegans, which grows in the wild in Brazilian forests, is a relatively unusual cultivated house plant. The flowers are about 10 cm (4 in) wide and appear from April to October according to the conditions the plant is kept in.

A. grandiflora, formerly known as *A. gigas,* has its natural habitat in the primary forests of Central America. Its stems climb to a height of 10 m (33 ft). It has very conspicuous, pipe-like blossoms, up to 35 cm (14 in) wide, which always attract attention.

Both species are demanding as regards temperature, humidity and space, and can be displayed only in a large tropical window. In winter they will grow at a temperature of 15 °C (59 °F).

The plants need regular watering adapted to seasonal changes, temperature of cultivation and light. Occasional feeding with a weak solution of a balanced fertilizer is recommended. Large plants can be cut back hard in spring because the flowers are borne on the new growths.

Warmth-loving species of *Aristolochia* are usually increased by cuttings. Softwood or stem cuttings root readily in a propagating frame with bottom heat kept at a temperature of 22 to 25 °C (71 to 77 °F). Propagation from seed is also possible.

2

Aristolochia elegans (1) is a less demanding and comparatively fast-growing species, suitable for indoor cultivation at a temperature up to 18 °C (64 °F). It flowers from April to October. Young plants are tied to a stick or other support. In a favourable site, an older plant will soon cover a large wall.

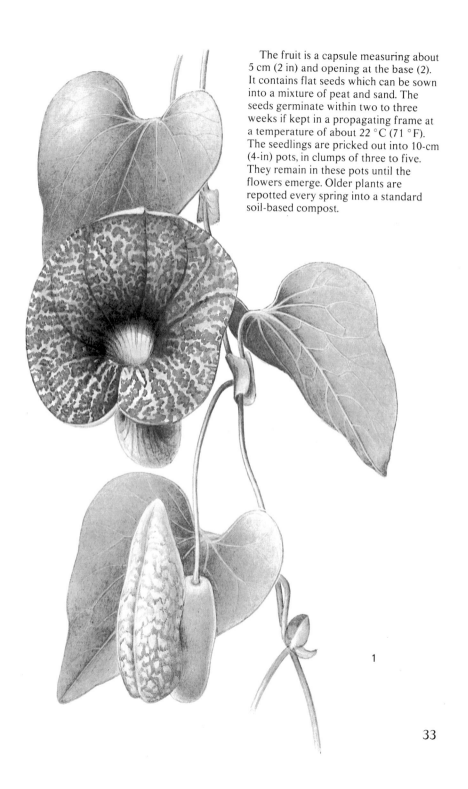

The fruit is a capsule measuring about 5 cm (2 in) and opening at the base (2). It contains flat seeds which can be sown into a mixture of peat and sand. The seeds germinate within two to three weeks if kept in a propagating frame at a temperature of about 22 °C (71 °F). The seedlings are pricked out into 10-cm (4-in) pots, in clumps of three to five. They remain in these pots until the flowers emerge. Older plants are repotted every spring into a standard soil-based compost.

1

Dutchman's Pipe
Aristolochia macrophylla   Aristolochiaceae

Aristolochia macrophylla, also referred to as *A. durior* or *A. sipho,* makes a good green covering for high walls facing north or west. It quickly forms a thick growth over a pergola, or wall almost impenetrable by light. The leaves, overlapping like shingles, entirely cover the construction and create an enclosed environment. *A. macrophylla* can also be trained over garden fences up a lamp post, over an old tree trunk, or up a chain hung from the upper branches of a tall tree.

This species is frost-resistant. It should be planted in nutrient-rich, rather moist soil and tolerates even deep shade. It stands up well to industrially polluted air. The large leaves transpire heavily and so this plant must not be allowed to dry out. In the spring the plants benefit from three applications of a balanced fertilizer at six-week intervals. It is not necessary to cut the plants back regularly; older plants can always be cut back in early spring.

Aristolochia macrophylla is readily propagated by layering one-year-old shoots. After a year, the rooted parts can be separated and transferred to new sites. Propagation by means of seeds is also possible; the seeds are sown in spring and covered with glass. The seedlings start slowly and should be left undisturbed for two years before being transplanted.

Aristolochia macrophylla (1) grows in the wild on the mountain slopes of North America, at heights of up to 1,500 m (49,000 ft). It is a twining woody plant and in European conditions it soon reaches a height of 6 to 10 m (20 to 33 ft). It has been cultivated in Europe for more than two centuries. The deciduous leaves are about 25 cm (10 in) wide and overlap like shingles. The pipe-shaped, inconspicuous blossoms (2) are often concealed by the foliage. They usually appear in May and June. The unmistakable fragrance attracts the pollinating insects inside the blossoms from which they cannot escape before the anthers split and shower them with pollen. The insects covered with pollen then fly to another flower and pollinate it.

The flowers give off a distinctive smell attracting insects but offensive to man. Even young plants can produce flowers.

1

2

Smilax
Asparagus asparagoides
Liliaceae

The genus *Asparagus* comprises some 300 species occurring mainly in the Mediterranean region, southern Africa and some parts of Asia. It is represented by herbs or sub-shrubs with erect or climbing stems. The thickened roots serve as storage organs. The leaves are reduced, stunted or modified into thorns. The function of leaves is taken over by tiny needle-like or leaf-like formations called cladodes or cladophylls.

Asparagus asparagoides, also known as *A. medeloides,* used to be commonly grown as a greenhouse foliage plant. The cut fronds were used for bouquets. At present it is mainly used as a potted plant in cooler interiors.

Young plants of *Asparagus setaceus* (the Asparagus Fern), also known as *A. plumosus,* are grown in large quantities for fine cut greenery. Only fairly old plants form the characteristic climbing stems. Propagation is mainly by division of thick clumps. *A. setaceus* 'Nanus' is more compact, it has spreading branches and only later forms climbing shoots. *A. setaceus* 'Tenuissimus' has more delicate cladophylls and the climbing stems appear at an even greater age. The fronds of *A. setaceus* are commonly used for bouquets and other flower arrangements and decorative purposes. If kept in a cool place, its cladophylls on cut fronds stay fresh for a longer time than in the other species.

Asparagus asparagoides (1) from the Cape Province has twining stems up to 2 m (6 ft) long. The cladodes are ovate, elongated, leathery, about 2.5 cm (1 in) long. It makes a good decorative potted plant. Because of its robust appearance it is added only to bouquets featuring showy flowers.

3

Asparagus setaceus (2) is more common. It is a South African climbing sub-shrub with distinctly thin, spreading branches, about 1 m (3 ½ ft) long. The leaves are modified into downcurved thorns, 2.5 to 5 cm (1 to 2 in) long. Flowering occurs in September and October.

Bowiea volubilis (3) is another South African plant from family Liliaceae. The long, ascending stem and inconspicuous greenish-white flowers on long stalks grow from a large, green bulb. A winter temperature of 4 to 6 °C (39 to 43 °F) is sufficient.

Asparagus Fern
Asparagus densiflorus   Liliaceae

Asparagus densiflorus, also known as *A. sprengeri,* is an indispensable plant for cut greenery. It is highly adaptable as a potted plant and suits most requirements indoors. In winter, in poor light, it prefers temperatures below 15 °C (59 °F). From May to the first frosts, it can be stood outdoors in its container.

Asparagus densiflorus is suitable for window and balcony boxes, mainly on the shaded side of the house, where its trailing shoots are attractive throughout summer in the company of other species of ornamental plants, such as begonias and fuchsias. It requires plenty of fresh air and benefits from a shower of rain; plants kept indoors all year long create only stunted shoots. The length of shoots and the colour of the foliage are enhanced by regular feeding. From November to the end of February, *A. densiflorus* needs a rest, so watering must be reduced and a temperature of around 8 to 10 °C (46 to 50 °F) provided. Some older shoots turn yellow and die down, but this is not serious. In March, when new growth begins, the plants are repotted into a standard soil- or peat-based compost, and the watering gradually increased.

Asparagus is propagated by division when repotting or from seed, usually in spring.

Asparagus densiflorus (1) is native to South Africa, but grows in the wild form in the Mediterranean as well. It is a much-branched sub-shrub with at first erect, but later trailing stems, reaching a length of up to 2 m (6 ½ ft). The cladodes are 12 to 30 mm (up to 1 in) long and only 2 mm (about ¹/₁₀ in) wide. Tiny flowers appear in summer and smell of coconuts. The fruits are berries containing one to three seeds. The racemose inflorescence of *A. densiflorus* (3) is either white or a delicate pink. The tiny flowers are followed by at first green berries which later become red, containing glossy black seeds.

Asparagus densiflorus 'Myersii' (also known as *A. meyeri* or *A. myersii*) (2) is a slow-growing plant of compact growth, requiring rather higher temperatures than the species.

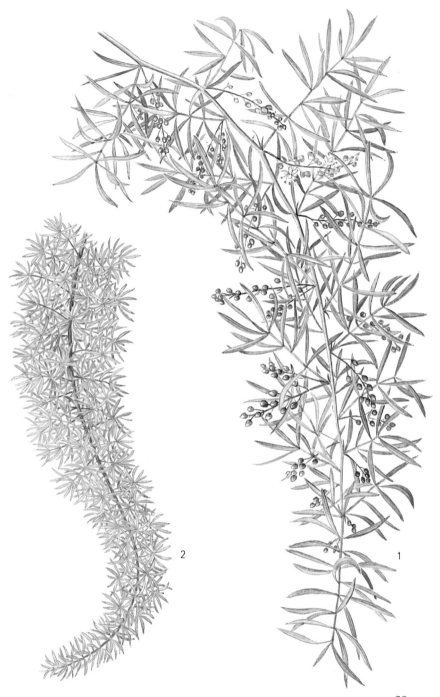

2

1

Begonia
Begonia limmingheana

Begoniaceae

Begonia limmingheana used to be a popular trailing plant. It can be planted in pots, or as a decorative plant in suspended containers. The plant sheds leaves if it is not getting enough water.

It should be given a position in good light indoors, but direct sunshine must be avoided. In a situation that is too shady the flowers will not develop their rich deep colour. In summer it does best at a temperature of 25 °C (77 °F), in winter at 20 °C (68 °F). When flower buds start forming, the plant requires an optimum temperature of 15 °C (59 °F); this temperature should be maintained for at least 50 days. This makes begonias suitable for controlled cultivation, and growers can thus supply flowering plants from November to May.

To prevent begonias from shedding their leaves, watering must be continued throughout winter. From March to August, a balanced liquid feed should be applied once a fortnight.

This species can be propagated from cuttings. The cuttings are taken from healthy stock plants grown at a temperature of at least 20 °C (77 °F). Three to five pieces are inserted into 8-cm (3-in) pots, and placed in a propagating frame. They root at an optimum temperature of 20 to 22 °C (68 to 71 °F). Later they should be transplanted into 10-cm (4-in) pots. The plants should start flowering within 8 months to a year.

Begonia limmingheana (1) is native to the forests of Brazil. It is a flowering shrub with trailing stems covered with leaves up to 13 cm (5 in) long. Loose inflorescences composed of a number of tiny blossoms appear from March to May.

Pellionia pulchra (2) is a trailing perennial that comes from Burma, Laos and Vietnam. The leaves are about 2.5 cm (1 in) long. It is an attractive ground-covering plant for a tropical greenhouse, centrally-heated home or closed flower window. It prefers shade and high humidity; the optimum temperature for cultivation is from 18 to 22 °C (64 to 71 °F).

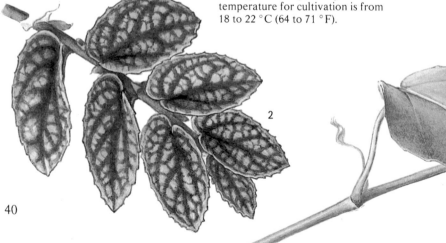

2

Pellionia daveauana (3) also
originates in south-eastern Asia. The
leaves measures 5 cm (2 in) long. Several
cultivars with different leaf patterning
have been bred from this species.

3

1

Paper Flower
Bougainvillea glabra
Nyctaginaceae

About 15 species of the genus *Bougainvillea* are found in forests and dry regions of South America. They are mostly thorny, climbing shrubs.

Bougainvilleas are grown in pots which in the summer can be placed outdoors on a terrace, balcony or in other suitable situations in the garden.

Bougainvillea glabra is a commonly cultivated, subtropical woody plant, which in the climatically favourable environment of the Mediterranean decorates fences, walls, pergolas and house walls. In the gardens of central Europe, it is grown in containers trained into tree-like forms. Its use as a house plant is less common. Luxuriantly growing cultivars can be planted in cool greenhouses, conservatories, closed glass porches, or in large flower windows.

In the summer, bougainvilleas require plenty of sunlight and regular watering, in the winter they make do with a temperature of 6 to 10 °C (43 to 50 ° F) and less watering. A six- to eight-week rest, during which watering is restricted to a minimum, is important for the plant to produce abundant flowers the following season. Normal watering is usually resumed in March. From April to the and of August, the plants must be fed once a fortnight with a balanced liquid fertilizer. In a warm and light position, bougainvilleas will flower almost all year round, although they bear the largest quantity of blossoms in the summer months when they get maximum sunlight.

3

2

Bougainvillea glabra (1) is found in the
wild in Brazil, reaching a height of up to
6 m (20 ft) and forming a large number of
small flowers supported by conspicuous
bracts. In the warmest regions of
southern Europe it is planted as a climber
in gardens and parks, and its flowering
period extends from spring to autumn. In
Britain it can be stood outside during the
summer.

The decorative character of this
climbing plant has drawn the attention of
many breeders of ornamental plants, and
new cultivars have appeared, having
more or less bright and deep-coloured
bracts and different sizes. *Bougainvillea
glabra* 'Sanderiana' is a smaller-sized
plant with deep mauve bracts (2). There
are also cultivars with flowers in various
shades of orange (3).

Bougainvillea
Bougainvillea × buttiana

Nyctaginaceae

Bougainvillea × buttiana is a hybrid of *B. glabra* and *B. peruviana,* usually flowering from April to June. Many cultivars, so far unnamed, have been bred from it; they produce pink, carmine, orange or scarlet bracts.

Bougainvillea spectabilis is another Brazilian species, similar to *B. × buttiana* but with larger, hairy leaves and vigorous growth. It is more demanding to grow as it needs greater warmth and is more particular with regards to soil. It flowers from April to July. Besides the species, there are cultivars with pink, red or orange bracts.

Young plants are transplanted every spring, older specimens once in two to four years. Plants should be repotted into containers only slightly bigger than the former pot and filled with an ericaceous soil-based compost. The optimum soil pH should be 6.0. Bougainvilleas need good drainage. When the flowers have withered, the plants can be cut back to encourage new shoots to form by winter as bougainvilleas flower on the previous year's wood. They usually shed their leaves in winter, but new ones grow at the beginning of the new season.

Propagation is by softwood cuttings taken in June, dipped in a hormone rooting powder and inserted into small pots filled with a mixture of peat and sand. These should be placed in a propagating frame with bottom heat and kept at a temperature of 25 to 30 °C (77 to 86 °F), they take root within three weeks.

4

2

From both its parents *Bougainvillea × buttiana* (1) inherited undemanding properties and a wide colour scale of bracts surrounding the tiny blossoms. It is usually grown in pots and tied to a stick or trained over an arched wire (2). The shoots of larger plants cultivated in greenhouses climb up plastic-coated wires, often reaching the roof. These

1

rewarding plants deserve to be given
more attention by growers.

New cultivars of bougainvillea have
been developed, some have creamy-white
bracts (4) or bracts of orange, pink,
carmine or scarlet shades (3). They are
slower growing, branch freely and are
more suitable for indoor cultivation in
pots.

3

45

Italian Bellflower
Campanula isophylla
Campanulaceae

Most of some 300 species of *Campanula* are found in the temperate or subtropical zones of the Northern Hemisphere, and they are grown in gardens as frost-resistant perennials. A single species — *Campanula isophylla* — has been a popular pot plant for a long time. It can be grown on window-sills as it is an undemanding plant. Because of its trailing habit, it can be used in various suspended containers or hanging baskets in cooler interiors or outside during the summer. During summer too, it can be grown in window boxes or in patio tubs in protected spots out of the wind. The pots have to be taken inside before the first frost.

    Campanula isophylla requires regular watering from spring to autumn, and a fortnightly liquid feed. Throughout winter it should be placed in a light spot with an optimum temperature of 10 °C (50 °F) and watering reduced. It is transplanted in the early spring, into a basic soil or peat-based compost. Older plants should be repotted once every two or three years.

    It is best propagated by division of thick clumps during transplanting. It can also be raised from softwood cuttings taken from healthy plants in February or March. Cuttings from non-flowering shoots, about 5 to 6 cm (2 to 2 1/4 in) long, take root in a mixture of peat and sand if kept at a temperature of 10 to 15 °C (50 to 59 °F), within four weeks.

2

Campanula isophylla grows wild in the rocky crevices of the limestone mountains in north-western Italy. The long, brittle stems creep along the ground, and from June to September are covered with masses of blossoms about 3.5 cm (1 1/2 in) wide. The species produces blue flowers and is called 'groom' (1).

    The cultivar *Campanula isophylla* 'Alba' has white flowers and is accordingly called 'bride' (2). The cultivar 'Mayi' has grey, downy leaves with a few white spots, and the flowers are pale blue.

1

The species and both cultivars require plenty of light in an open window and some protection from scorching sun. They do well in the shade but flower less profusely. In the summer months, bellflowers look attractive when displayed in hanging baskets.

47

Trumpet Vine, Trumpet Creeper
Campsis radicans
Bignoniaceae

The genus *Campsis* includes only two species and one inter-species hybrid. These loosely twining shrubs cling to the support with their adventitious roots and produce flowers on new wood, usually from July to September. They do well in a warm and sheltered garden, preferably on a south-facing wall. They need deep, humus-rich, well-drained and slightly alkaline soil. They are easily damaged by heavy frost but readily grow new shoots on lower parts. Until their first flowering, young plants may need winter protection if planted in an exposed or northern garden. Shoots are pruned after leaf fall in February or March.

Campsis radicans is a comparatively undemanding plant. Its tubular flowers are highly decorative and give an exotic touch to the garden. It is one of the best woody plants for covering a pergola in the south of the country. Despite being a slow grower in the first two years, it catches up rapidly once it has established itself.

Campsis grandiflora originates in Japan and China. It reaches a height of 3 to 6 m (10 to 20 ft). The flowers are larger than in *C. radicans,* scarlet with a carmine sheen, opening in August and September. It needs a protected, sunny position to do well.

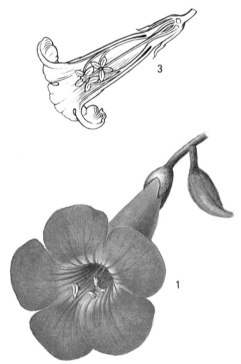

Campsis radicans was in the past classified in various genera, and it may still occasionally be found under the names of *Bignonia radicans* or *Tecoma radicans.* It is native to North America, occurring from California to Virginia. In Europe it reaches a height of about 8 m (26 ft). The flower tube is 5 to 8 cm (2 to 3 in) long. The species (1) is most commonly grown in gardens as it is hardier than the cultivars. The cultivars available are 'Atropurpurea' (2) with a deep red tube, 'Praecox' with a scarlet tube, and 'Flora' which has yellow flowers.

The flowers of Trumpet Vines (illustration 3 shows a cross-section) grow in multi-flowered panicles at the tips of new shoots. They emerge in late summer and need plenty of sun. The tube composed of five fused petals soon withers and only a scar remains on the flower stalk.

2

A young plant has to be tied to the
support before it is able to hold to it by
means of numerous aerial roots, which
are formed only on the side of the stem
away from the sun (4).

4

Trumpet Vine, Trumpet Creeper
Campsis × *tagliabuana*

Bignoniacae

Campsis × *tagliabuana* is a hybrid between *C. radicans* and *C. grandiflora.* The plants are distinguished according to their predominant features: some are good climbers, others are of shrubby habit. Resistance to frost also varies.

Trumpet vines are propagated mainly by layering. *Campsis radicans* tends to produce a multitude of root suckers, which are often undesirable. Cultivars are grafted on the stocks of this species planted in pots; grafting is done in a greenhouse in winter. Propagation by root cuttings is an alternative method. The cuttings are set out in autumn when they are 8 cm (3 in) long and 2.5 cm (1 in) thick. They produce new growths in the following year and are tied to sticks. In early spring, seeds of the species can be sown in seed trays kept in a propagating frame, preferably with some bottom heat.

In the Mediterranean, these climbers are found in almost every street. But in most of Britain, if conditions are not too exposed, Trumpet Vines can brighten garden gates or walls. They can climb posts or be trained up trellis. They have to be tied firmly, because even large plants can snap easily in a strong wind. Cut flowers do not last long.

Campsis × *tagliabuana* has given rise to many cultivars, the most commonly available being *C.* × *tagliabuana* 'Madame Galen' (1) producing abundant flowers and tolerating central European winters. Although the plants produce a great number of adventitious roots, they need to be tied to a support, at least at first.

3   2

1

Breeding of Trumpet Vines has recently become popular with growers, and many new cultivars have been raised with flowers in various shades of red, orange, pink and yellow. The pink ones include *C.* × *tagliabuana* 'Rosea' (2) and the yellow ones *C.* × *tagliabuana* 'Yellow Trumpet' (3). However, their colours have not yet achieved such perfection so as to compete with the orange-red cultivars and they are extremely difficult to get hold of.

51

Climbing Bittersweet
Celastrus scandens
Celastraceae

There are about 30 known species of this genus. They grow in the wild in Asia, America, Australia and southern Africa. A single wild species is found in Spain. These are twining shrubs with deciduous leaves. In the wild they are usually dioecious, but specimens with separate male and female flowers also occur.

Only a few species of *Celastrus* are cultivated in European gardens. They are relatively undemanding plants and do well in most soils. They do equally well in sunny and semi-shaded situations.

Celastrus scandens is a North American climber which can be allowed to scale the trunk of a tall tree, a pillar or arch. It is an undemanding woody plant tolerating semi-shade and polluted atmospheres.

Celastrus orbiculatus is native to China and Japan. Under favourable conditions it can reach a height of up to 12 m (40 ft). The leaves are almost 10 cm (4 in) long and turn a beautiful yellow in the autumn. It prefers a sunny site.

Celastrus does not require regular pruning. It can be propagated by layering, taking root cuttings or lifting root suckers, which often become so numerous, especially in *C. orbiculatus*, that they become a nuisance. Seeds are sown in April after stratification (exposing the seeds to a period of frost to hasten germination).

Members of this genus need support and should therefore be planted against a pergola, fence or wall.

1

2

3

Celastrus scandens is 6 to 9 m (20 to 30 ft) tall. It is found in the wild throughout the eastern parts of North America. In June it produces tiny blossoms in terminal inflorescences (1). The leaves are deciduous but the fruits when formed persist. The latter are decorative but poisonous.

Celastrus orbiculatus flowers in late May and June, but the blossoms are insignificant (2). After pollination, the female flowers develop into pea-sized, scarlet fruits in yellow coatings (3), and these persist until winter. The branches with fruits can be cut after ripening, stored in a dry place and used in flower arrangements together with some dried annuals and branches of conifers.

53

Hearts Entangled, Rosary Vine
Ceropegia woodii
Asclepiadaceae

The genus *Ceropegia* includes some 155 species, found in the wild in Africa, Asia and Australia. They are mostly herbs of climbing or trailing habit.

The most common in cultivation is *Ceropegia woodii,* formerly known as *C. linearis* ssp. *woodii* or *C. hastata.* It is native to south-eastern Africa.

This species requires a light but not too warm position. Being a succulent, it withstands the dry air of modern homes with central heating. It needs regular watering from April to September, and a fortnightly application of liquid fertilizer. Watering must be reduced during the other months. In winter, the plants should be kept at a minimum temperature of 10 °C (50 °F). Mature plants are transplanted, preferably early in spring, once in two or three years if they have filled their pots with roots.

Propagation is by stem cuttings which can be taken any time of the year. Each cutting should have at least two pairs of leaves. Several cuttings can be put together in a pot filled with light, sandy soil. In a propagating frame at a temperature of 15 to 20 °C (59 to 68 °F) they usually take root within four to six weeks.

Ceropegia can be tied to a decorative bamboo trellis, but it will look more natural on an epiphytic trunk, or situated on a shelf with its long stems hanging down freely.

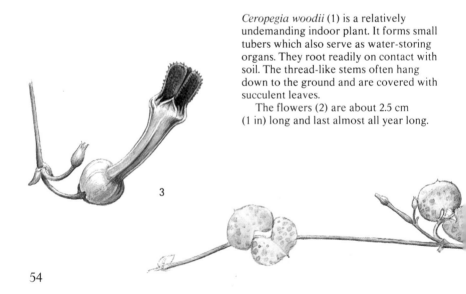

Ceropegia woodii (1) is a relatively undemanding indoor plant. It forms small tubers which also serve as water-storing organs. They root readily on contact with soil. The thread-like stems often hang down to the ground and are covered with succulent leaves.

The flowers (2) are about 2.5 cm (1 in) long and last almost all year long.

Their shape resembles slender oriental lanterns. Insects are attracted to the flowers by their bizarre shapes and a peculiar scent. The pollinator crawls inside the flower but cannot leave before the hairs inside wither to open the way out. In the meantime, the insects transfer pollen from anthers to the stigma.

Ceropegia distincta (3) has up to 35 mm long, cream-white flowers with brown spots; they form a sparse inflorescence and open successively from June to August.

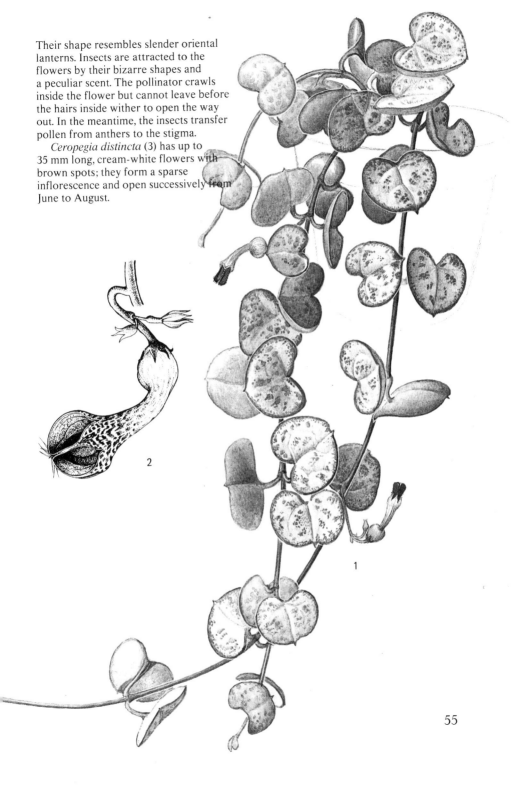

2

1

Kangaroo Vine
Cissus antarctica
Vitaceae

Some 300 species of this genus are found in the tropical and subtropical regions of Australia, America, Africa and Polynesia. Only a few of them are cultivated indoors. These are mostly evergreen climbers with twining tendrils.

Cissus antarctica is usually tied to a decorative support or it can be trained up a trellis to cover a wall in a cool spot, such as a hallway, landing or stairwell. High temperatures cause the leaves to turn brown and fall off.

Kangaroo Vines rank among the hardiest and most undemanding of house plants. The optimum temperature in winter is 12 to 15 °C (53 to 59 °F), but plants stand up to temperatures just above freezing for short periods. They tolerate the dry air of centrally-heated homes and do well both in full light and semi-shade.

In summer, cissus can be stood outside on a balcony or in the garden, provided it is sheltered from direct sunshine, at least at noon. Watering must be adapted to season and light intensity. The roots must never be allowed to dry out even in winter to prevent leaf shedding. During full growth, from April to September, the plants benefit from an application of liquid fertilizer once a fortnight. Repot in spring using a standard soil- or peat-based compost. Hydroponics is another successful method of cultivating this plant. Cissus proves to be an almost ideal plant for beginners.

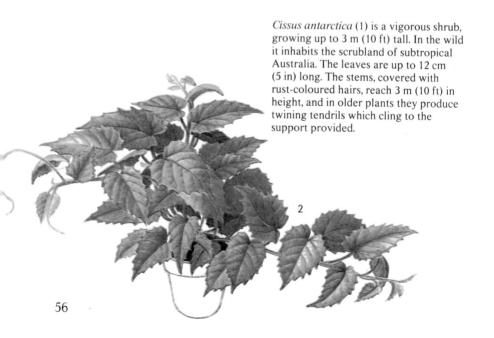

Cissus antarctica (1) is a vigorous shrub, growing up to 3 m (10 ft) tall. In the wild it inhabits the scrubland of subtropical Australia. The leaves are up to 12 cm (5 in) long. The stems, covered with rust-coloured hairs, reach 3 m (10 ft) in height, and in older plants they produce twining tendrils which cling to the support provided.

2

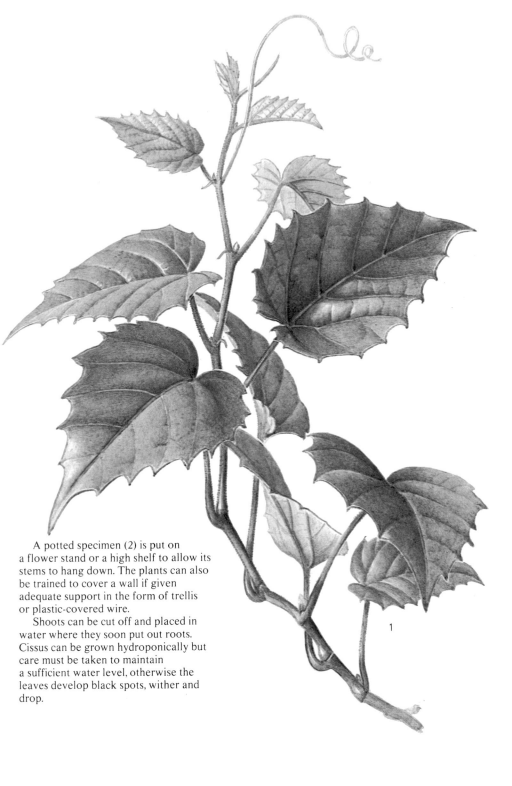

A potted specimen (2) is put on
a flower stand or a high shelf to allow its
stems to hang down. The plants can also
be trained to cover a wall if given
adequate support in the form of trellis
or plastic-covered wire.

Shoots can be cut off and placed in
water where they soon put out roots.
Cissus can be grown hydroponically but
care must be taken to maintain
a sufficient water level, otherwise the
leaves develop black spots, wither and
drop.

1

Begonia Vine
Cissus discolor
Vitaceae

Cissus discolor is an evergreen climber growing in the humid tropical forests of Java. The variegated leaves are up to 15 cm (6 in) long and 8 cm (3 in) wide.

This pot plant is suitable for a warm greenhouse. But it is difficult to grow in the home, except perhaps in a closed flower window or a vitrine. It requires a position in light shade, a constant temperature of about 20 °C (68 °F) throughout the winter and high atmospheric humidity, otherwise the leaves will soon wither. During the summer months water well and feed regularly. The roots must never become too dry, even in winter.

The plants are propagated by means of stem cuttings bearing two pairs of leaves. They are inserted into a mixture of peat and sharp sand, three to five cuttings to a pot. Young plants can be tied to sticks to train them upwards or they can be grown as trailing plants.

This attractive foliage plant is frequently used by florists in gift baskets and mixed plant arrangements fot short-term effect. It should, however, never stay in the basket for long, but be transplanted into a pot and situated in a place corresponding to its requirements of temperature and humidity. This is important for successfully keeping a Begonia Vine.

Cissus discolor (1) is grown for its highly decorative foliage. The thin stems produce tendrils which cling to available supports. Maintaining the attractive colours of the foliage depends mainly on the light intensity; the most beautiful shades develop in late spring and early summer. For short-term purposes, this species can be sunk in a bowl and used together with other ornamental plants in a mixed arrangement; the trailing shoots must cover the edges of the container. If the leaves start to drop in winter, watering should be restricted to a minimum and the plant kept in the same spot and not moved around; new growths should appear in spring.

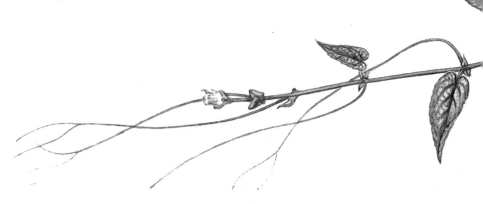

1

Grape Ivy, Natal Vine
Rhoicissus rhomboidea

Vitaceae

Rhoicissus rhomboidea, often listed under the name of *Cissus rhombi-folia*, is native to South Africa. It is an easy-going plant, succeeding both in the sun and shade. In summer it can be placed outside a balcony or garden terrace, while in winter it prefers a light position and an optimum temperature of 10 to 15 °C (50 to 59 °F). It tolerates occasional temperature of 10 °C (39 °F) and dislikes winter temperatures above 16 °C (60 °F).

Watering must be adjusted according to the temperature and to the season; plenty of water in a hot summer, occasional watering in cool weather. If the roots become too dry or too moist, the plant sheds its leaves. Feed fortnightly from April to July. Any cutting back and repotting is carried out in spring, older specimens only need repotting once in two or three years; a soil- or peat-based compost will suit these plants equally well.

Propagation is by cuttings, preferably taken in February and March, or in August. Ripened shoots are used. Softwood cuttings must be about 10 cm (4 in) long, cuttings must have two buds each. Three to five cuttings are inserted into a 8-cm (3-in) pot filled with a cutting compost. When kept in a propagating frame at a temperature of 22 to 23 °C (71 to 73 °F), roots develop within three to four weeks.

2

Rhoicissus rhomboidea (1) is a popular and undemanding vine. It can be trained up sticks or trellis, or used in hanging baskets. Young stems and leaf stalks are brown and covered with felt-like hairs. The inflorescence is unimpressive and it is grown as a foliage plant.

A new cultivar has been commonly grown recently: *Rhoicissus rhomboidea* 'Ellen Danica' (2) with attractively cut leaves and lush growth.

Cissus striata (3) originates in southern Brazil and Chile. The evergreen leaves are composed of individual leaflets, 2.5 to 5 cm (1 to 2 in) long. This species likes cool conditions and is used in hanging baskets or containers which display its trailing branches.

Cissus discolor mollis

Cissus discolor mollis, also referred to as *C. velutina,* is a relatively little-known cissus which should be grown in warm greenhouses.

Many other interesting cissus species, e. g. *Cissus amazonica,* can be found in botanical gardens or in specialized collections. This climbing perennial from the Amazon River basin has long, thin stems with a brownish-green sheen and elongated, oval, up to 10 cm (4 in) long leaves, grey-green with a silvery venation and almost red undersides. It requires a temperature of about 20 °C (68 °F), constant humidity, regular feeding during the summer months and a position in semi-shade.

Cissus gongylodes is a climber native to Brazil, Paraguay and Peru. It has thick, angular, hairy stems which become reddish provided the plant receives plenty of light. The trimerous leaves have a blade up to 30 cm (12 in) long and a winged petiole. The plant produces a number of aerial roots, it is extremely rampant and tolerates dry air.

Cissus njegerre comes from the mountain forests of eastern Africa. The leaves are trimerous, long-elliptical, highly wrinkled, covered with fine red hairs. It should be grown in a warm greenhouse but it tolerates dry air. It flowers profusely under favourable conditions.

Cissus quadrangularis originates in tropical Africa, Arabian Peninsula, India, Indonesia and the Philippines. It is a robust liana with angular stems, thickened in some places, and tiny, deciduous leaves. It requires warmth, high humidity and partial shade.

Cissus discolor mollis (1) climbs to a height of about 5 m (16 ft). Its long and thin stems are sparsely covered with soft leaves. As to cultivation, it has similar requirements as *C. discolor;* it must be placed in a heated greenhouse, heated conservatory or tropical window with high humidity and in semi-shade. A temperature of 15 to 18 °C (59 to 64 °F) is best in winter.

Under favourable conditions *Cissus discolor mollis* flowers regularly in late summer, although the blossoms are not very impressive (2). It is propagated by softwood cuttings raised under glass.

Three to five cuttings are inserted into 8-cm (3-in) pots and placed in a propagating frame with bottom heat. The young plants are potted on into larger pots as necessary.

1

63

Clematis alpina

The genus *Clematis* comprises some 230 species, predominantly of climbing or trailing habit. They include shrubs, sub-shrubs and perennials. Their homeland is mainly the temperate zones of Europe and Asia.

Clematis alpina was formerly classified in another genus under the name of *Atragene alpina.* It is found on rocky slopes in the Alps, Carpathians, Caucasus, and in Siberia and Scandinavia. It is more of a creeper than a climber.

This is not a very strong-growing species and can be best displayed scrambling over a large rock òr stone wall. It looks most effective where the stems can creep over bigger stones or climb the branches of shrubs or small trees. The stems can also be trained over lower wire fencing surrounding the garden.

Clematis alpina is readily propagated from seeds sown in mid-March following stratification. The seedlings grow in a greenhouse or cold frame and later are transferred outdoors to a slightly shady spot. The seeds germinate within four to five weeks.

This native of open woodlands and shrub-covered slopes needs shade to protect its roots, although the parts of the plant above the ground grow well in sunshine or semi-shade. The plants need a humus-rich, well drained but moist soil.

Clematis alpina (1) has stems about 2 m (6 ft) long, and the trimerous leaves are 5 cm (3 in) long and 2.5 cm (1 in) wide. The flowers are 4 to 6 cm (1 ½ to 2 ¼ in) across. If situated in a favourable position, the plant produces flowers on the previous year's wood in April and May. A pleasant fragrance is particularly characteristic of the pink-flowered forms. The seedheads with their long silky appendages are also highly decorative. This species shows great variety in the colour of its flowers and has attracted the attention of clematis breeders.

2

3

The best known cultivars include
Clematis alpina sibirica with
creamy-white flowers (2), *C. a.* 'Frances
Rivis' with blue flowers, and *C. a* 'Ruby'
with pink-red flowers (3). Double-flowered
cultivars have been obtained by
cross-breeding with *C. macropetala.*

1

Mountain Clematis
Clematis montana   Ranunculaceae

The natural distribution of *Clematis montana* is on the slopes of the Himalayas at heights of up to 3,000 m (9,850 ft). In its homeland it often surpasses 10 m (33 ft) in height. The species was introduced to Britain in 1831. The species is still cultivated, but its varieties or cultivars with pink, red, lilac or white flowers are grown more widely. Some have bronze-coloured foliage or reddish shoots.

Clematis montana is a very undemanding, climbing woody plant clinging to any support by means of leaf stalks up to 8 cm (3 in) long. In a harsh winter, the plant sometimes suffers but quickly grows new shoots again. The flowers are borne on the previous year's growth, and pruning must be done after the flowering. As with *C. alpina,* the roots should be in a cool damp position, preferably under stone slabs laid on the earth.

This species is used to cover house walls or high fences, especially on the shaded side of the house. Because of their rampant growth, the plants cover a large area in a couple of years. They can also be trained over pergolas, dividing walls or trunks of tall trees.

The species can be raised from seed, varieties and cultivars are propagated only by vegetative methods. Layering is recommended in gardens.

1

Clematis montana (1) bears white flowers in May and June. The flowers are about 5 cm (2 in) across and give off a faint perfume. The species shows an enormous variety of shades of colour and shapes of flower. There are many varieties; *C. m. grandiflora* has pink-flushed, white flowers up to 8 cm (3 in) across. *C. m. rubens* has flowers 5 to 6 cm (2 to 2 1/4 in) across, pinkish-red,

appearing in May and June (2), and
C. m. wilsonii has small white blossoms
borne in June and July. Popular cultivars
include 'Alexander', scented with
creamy-white flowers, and 'Tetrarose',
having deep pink flowers, up to 7.5 cm
(nearly 3 in) across. Breeding still
continues and new cultivars with
improved qualities appear every year.

2

Clematis tangutica

Clematis tangutica is another favourite climbing plant found in parks and gardens. It is quite hardy. It is effective in informal areas of the garden, especially if allowed to climb over large shrubs. It has many uses: it can cover a chicken-wire fence or trellis, be trained to cover a wall or creep over large stones in the rock garden. It is appreciated for its golden-yellow blossoms, an unusual colour in this genus. It is undemanding and resists diseases like the other species of *Clematis*. Cultivation is the same as for *C. montana,* any cutting back is undertaken in late winter as the flowers are carried on new wood.

The Vine Bower, *Clematis viticella,* is another species grown in parks or gardens. It is native to south-eastern Europe. It reaches a height of about 4 m (13 ft). The wide, bell-shaped, pinkish-violet flowers, measuring up to 5 cm (2 in) across, appear from July to September. The cultivars include 'Alba Luxurians' with white flowers, the double-flowered blue-violet 'Purpurea', 'Kermesina' with red flowers and 'Royal Velours' with deep purple flowers. This is a relatively hardy and very vigorous species, but it has to be tied to a support. It flowers on new wood and should be hard pruned in spring.

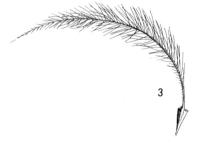

3

2

Clematis tangutica (1) is a native of Tibet, Mongolia and south-western China. It reaches a height of up to 6 m (20 ft) in the wild, but 3 m (10 ft) is more usual in cultivation. The bell-shaped blossoms are 3.5 to 7 cm (1 1/2 to 2 3/4 in) across. The flowering period is relatively long, as the first flowers emerge in July and flowering continues until October.

68

1

After flowering the plant displays
attractive clusters of seedheads (2) which
persist through most of the winter. These
seedheads are silvery green at first and
grey-brown in winter. They are composed
of achenes with feathery appendages (3).

Traveller's Joy
Clematis vitalba

The Traveller's Joy is one of the most luxuriantly growing plants of hedgerow and countryside. It also occurs in deciduous woods, thickets and on river banks. It is also common in northern Africa and the Caucasus. This undemanding plant is completely hardy. On the other hand, it does not tolerate very dry sites. Because of its rampant growth, it is rarely planted in a garden, but it is effective in country areas where it can mask an old fence or climb up to the crown of a tall tree. A chain, wire or rope can be hung from the branches of a large, strong-growing tree, and the shoots will climb up to the sun. It rapidly multiplies itself by self-sowing if grown in a favourable spot.

Clematis species and their varieties are usually small-flowered, of vigorous growth and producing more blossoms than the garden cultivars. They also suffer less from diseases and need not be tied in position; some reach treetops or cover a large wall or slope in a short time. For aesthetic reasons, several species of differing vigour should never be planted out together as the weaker plants will be swamped. When setting out a clematis against a pergola or other construction, the weight of the plant must be taken into account and a sufficiently solid construction chosen accordingly.

Clematis vitalba (1) usually reaches a height of 10 to 12 m (33 to 40 ft), but it can grow even taller if placed in a favourable site. Its creamy-white flowers, measuring up to 2 cm (3/4 in) across, bloom in July and August and give off a pleasant smell of bitter almonds.

Like other species of *Clematis,* the petals are absent and substituted by enlarged and attractively coloured sepals (2). The flowers are followed by numerous feathery seedheads which turn from silver at first to grey. The achenes

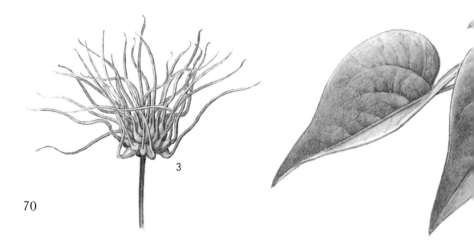

3

contain tiny pits and after ripening carry
long feathery appendages (4). The
seedheads of Traveller's Joy are
extremely decorative (3). In autumn and
winter they are frequently used in flower
arrangements.

2

4

1

71

Jackmanii Section
Clematis
Ranunculaceae

Large-flowered cultivars of clematis originating from cross-breeding of *Clematis florida, C. × jackmanii, C. lanuginosa, C. patens, C. texensis, C. viticella* and other species are listed under the garden hybrids. Although they rarely reach the height of the species, their flowers are considerably larger and of more vivid hues. They are classified in several sections according to the species which predominated in their breeding history.

The Jackmanii section includes cultivars having external features and qualities similar to the hybrid *C. × jackmanii*, which is a result of cross-breeding between *C. lanuginosa* and *C. viticella*.

Clematis × jackmanii, the oldest large-flowered hybrid, was bred by Messrs Jackman of Woking around 1860, and it has been one of the most common cultivars of large-flowered hybrid clematis ever since. It attains a height of 3 to 4 m (10 to 13 ft). The flowers are borne on the new wood, usually from June to September, but single blossoms may appear later. The flowers are purple-violet, 10 to 12 cm (4 to 4 ½ in) across, long-stalked, with normally four spreading sepals. *C. × jackmanii* is extremely hardy. Young plants should be tied to a stick, older specimens will hold onto a wire-netting fence, trellis or other garden feature.

Clematis × jackmanii (1) has been used to breed a number of cultivars with saucer- or bowl-shaped flowers. The flowers are up to 20 cm (8 in) across, with four to eight sepals and growing in twos or threes on long petioles. The most common cultivars include 'Comtesse de Bouchard' with pinkish-red flowers (2);

3

1

2

'Gipsy Queen', rich purple-blue;
'Jackmanii Superba', mauve-blue; 'Perle
d'Azure', bright blue with striping (3).
and 'The President' with deep
purple-blue flowers and dark brownish
stamens. All cultivars have long-lasting
flowers, which stand up well to rainy
weather. They can be cut but will not last
long in the vase.

Lanuginosa Section
Clematis
Ranunculaceae

This section comprises cultivars based mainly on *Clematis lanuginosa*, a native of central and eastern China. Garden cultivars of the Lanuginosa section are vigorous growers and excellent subjects for covering columns or archways of garden gates. They are also effective on trellis or light fences. The roots require shading which can be obtained by planting a protective layer of low shrubs and perennials, or situating a boulder or stone slab to shade the roots at noon. Annual mulching is advisable, using peat, well-rotted compost or forest bark.

The Florida section displays the influence of the Japanese species, *Clematis florida*, which can be damaged in severe winters. Both the species and the cultivars grow to a maximum height of 3 m (10 ft). They flower less profusely than *C. lanuginosa* but the flowers are much larger. *C. florida* produces white blossoms during June and July. The flowers are borne on new wood, and therefore *C. florida* should be pruned in early spring. The most common cultivars are 'Belle of Woking', full-flowered with white, silvery sepals, 'Duchess of Edinburgh' with large, double white flowers, and the semi-double purple-pink 'Proteus'.

3

2

74

Clematis lanuginosa is about 2 m (6 ft) high and bears a multitude of flowers. The cultivars have fewer flowers than the species but produce them in succession from May to September or October. The flowers have six to eight sepals, mostly pale shades. Some cultivars flower early on the previous year's wood, others on new shoots, so pruning has to be timed accordingly. The best known cultivars

include: 'Blue Gem' with azure-blue flowers (2); 'Crimson King', claret-red with brown stamens; 'Henryi', pure white; 'Nelly Moser', pinkish-white with a carmine stripe down each sepal and red stamens (1); 'Sensation', satiny-mauve red; 'W. E. Gladstone', large-flowered, lilac-blue with fine striping; and 'William Kennet' with deep lavender blossoms. The seedheads of the cultivars (3) are less attractive than those of the species.

Patens Section
Clematis Ranunculaceae

Cultivars of the Patens section are rather more demanding as regards soil and cultivation than the other clematis sections. The soil should be ideally a loam, rich in humus and nutrients, slightly alkaline and well-drained. A good mulch of well-rotted compost or farmhouse manure applied every autumn will ensure a good display of flowers each year.

The species that has given rise to these cultivars is *Clematis patens* from Japan. It is relatively vigorous in growth, reaching 3 to 4 m (10 to 13 ft) in height. The flowers are borne on old wood, usually in May and June. They measure 10 to 15 cm (4 to 6 in) across and open in succession. The plants are rather more tender than other clematis and are best grown in a sheltered position.

The best months for planting clematis are April and May. Since they are usually sold in containers, however, they can be set out any time from spring to autumn. The graft should be buried some 10 cm (4 in) underground, otherwise the scion might be damaged by frost or pests and only the stock will sprout. A newly-planted specimen can be pruned some 30 cm (12 in) above the ground to promote branching out.

Garden hybrids are grafted on root stocks of *Clematis viticella* in a greenhouse or frame in late February. They can also be raised from softwood cuttings taken in July from half-ripe shoots, trimmed to 3 to 4 cm (about 1 ½ in), dipped in hormone rooting powder and placed in a propagating frame. They take root within four to six weeks. Private gardeners usually increase clematis by layering.

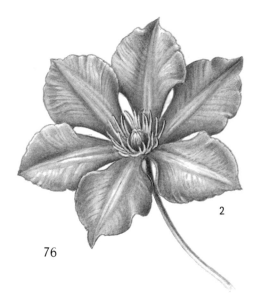

2

Cultivars of the Patens section usually have six sepals. There are many cultivars, and only the most common will be mentioned. Recommended cultivars are 'Barbara' with violet flowers with carmine stripes; 'Daniel Deronda', purple-blue with yellow stamens; 'Fair Rosamund', pink with deeper stripes, mauve stamens;

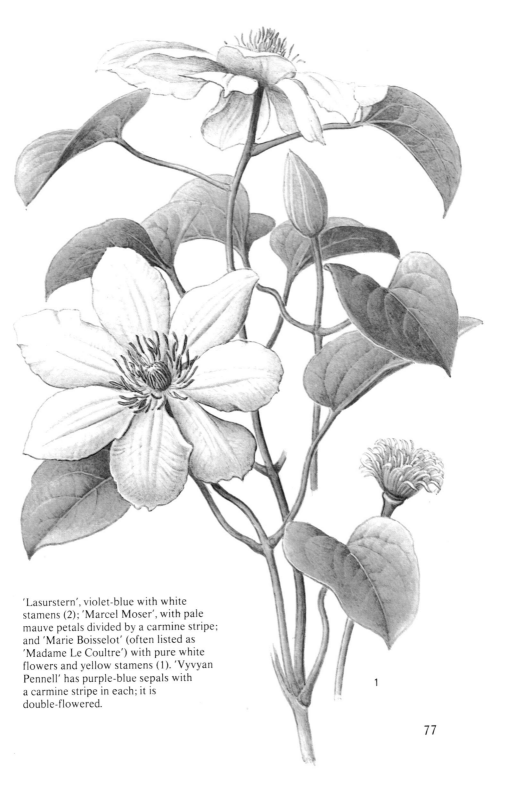

'Lasurstern', violet-blue with white
stamens (2); 'Marcel Moser', with pale
mauve petals divided by a carmine stripe;
and 'Marie Boisselot' (often listed as
'Madame Le Coultre') with pure white
flowers and yellow stamens (1). 'Vyvyan
Pennell' has purple-blue sepals with
a carmine stripe in each; it is
double-flowered.

1

Glory Bower, Bleeding Heart Vine
Clerodendrum thomsoniae   Verbenaceae

Over 275 species of this genus originate in central Africa and in the primary forests of tropical and subtropical Asia.

The rampant climbing woody *Clerodendrum thomsoniae* is native to western Africa. Flowering usually occurs from April to June, but flowers appear in smaller quantities outside this period as well. In summer the plants thrive at a temperature of 20 to 22 °C (68 to 71 °F) and require high humidity and partial shade. From December to February they undergo a period of relative rest and prefer lower temperatures of 12 to 15 °C (53 to 59 °F) and a reduction in watering, otherwise the plants will not flower the following year.

During full growth, regular watering is very important and leaves should be mist-sprayed frequently. A liquid fertilizer should be applied every two weeks from April to August. The growth increases as the temperature rises, but lower temperatures promote flowering. Most leaves are shed in winter and the plants can be hard pruned in February, or repotted.

Propagation is usually carried out in February from hardwood cuttings, some 8 to 10 cm (3 to 4 in) long. Three to five cuttings are inserted in a 8-cm (3-in) pot, filled with peat and sand. In a propagating frame with bottom heat, they usually put out roots in two to three weeks. Softwood cuttings can be taken in mid-spring. The shoots of young plants are tied to sticks, later trained over plastic-covered wire arches or trellis.

2

Clerodendrum thomsoniae (1) has been grown in Britain and Europe as a house plant for cool interiors for over a century. Smaller plants are grown in pots, larger specimens are placed in a greenhouse, conservatory or hallway with fairly humid air. A large plant can create an attractive flowering screen for a room divide or other construction. Young plants have to be pinched back repeatedly to encourage branching.

The narrow, tubular flowers consist of five petals and three sepals. They resemble paper lanterns by their shape and arrangement (2).

1

Cup-and-saucer Plant
Cobaea scandens
Polemoniaceae

The genus *Cobaea* consists of nine species found in the wild in tropical Latin America. The main ornamental species grown is the annual *Cobaea scandens.* It is native to Mexico and Costa Rica, where it attains a height of 12 m (40 ft). However, in the most favourable climatic conditions of Britain it only reaches a height of around 6 m (20 ft).

Cobaea scandens requires well-drained, rich loamy soil. It tolerates semi-shade but produces more flowers in the sun. It has a large leaf surface, which transpires profusely in hot weather so the plant needs abundant and regular watering.

The seeds are sown under glass or in a propagating frame in February or March. At a temperature of 15 to 20 °C (59 to 68 °F) they germinate within 10 to 20 days and can soon be pricked out into pots. A stick should be inserted at an early stage for support. The seedlings are grown on at a temperature of 12 to 15 °C (53 to 59 °F). The young plants can be set out in their outdoor growing positions in late May, spaced about 80 cm (32 in) apart. Propagation can also be done from cuttings taken from overwintered plants growing in a greenhouse, preferably in March. The plants grown from cuttings tend to flower earlier.

This fast-growing annual is planted against a wall, pergola, trellis or balcony rail. When grown in a container it rarely surpasses 2 m (6 ft) in height.

Cobaea scandens (1) has flexible stems, twining readily and easily clinging to wire netting. It produces flowers according to the time the plants were raised, usually from mid-July to October. The bell-shaped flowers are 5 to 6 cm (2 to 2 ¼ in) across. Young plants have to be tied to sticks, older ones to trellis or training wires. They can also be taped to a wall.

In addition to the species, which has greenish flowers later turning dark violet, there are cultivars producing white (2) or blue (3) flowers. Growers should bear in mind that the flowers are short-lived and disappear with the onset of chilly autumn weather.

1

2

3

Columnea hirta

Some 125 species have been discovered in tropical Latin America. They are epiphytes growing on trees or in rocky crevices.

Columnea hirta, a native of Costa Rica, is a common indoor plant. Its branches are closely packed with leaves about 2.5 cm (1 in) long. Flowering occurs between March and May. *C. gloriosa,* also native to Costa Rica, is found in the wild in warm, humid forests. The leaves are about 4.5 cm (1 ¾ in) long. The flower is tubular and up to 10 cm (4 in) long, a delicate red with a yellow inside. It flowers from November to May. The cultivar *C. gloriosa* 'Purpurea' has bronze-red foliage.

Columnea microphylla, another Costa Rican species, has smallish leaves, only about 1 cm (½ in) long. The shining orange flowers, up to 8 cm (3 in) long, appear from March to August.

All these species of the genus *Columnea* are demanding as to temperature and humidity. They do well in a light position out of direct sunshine. Watering should be moderate but regular. Flower buds are formed in a six-week rest period in winter, when plants are kept at a temperature of 12 to 15 °C (53 to 59 °F), and watering is reduced.

Propagation is done in spring: stem cuttings with two to three pairs of leaves are inserted in 8-cm (3-in) pots filled with a mixture of coarse sand and peat, three to five cuttings per pot. In a propagating frame kept at a temperature of 20 to 25 °C (68 to 77 °F), the roots will form within two to three weeks.

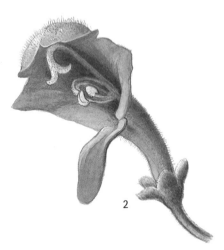

2

Columnea hirta (1) is an evergreen like the other species; care has to be taken to prevent the loss of leaves. If this happens the temperature, watering and light have to be adapted to provide a more favourable environment. The optimum soil ph is 4.5, which means that this plant will not tolerate lime. It thrives in a heated greenhouse, conservatory or vitrine, planted on an attractive piece of wood where its long trailing branches can be displayed to good effect.

The flowers (2) have a long and tubular corolla, often with longish lips. There is a small yellow spot in the throat. Columnea does better without fertilizers; well-fed plants grow vigorously but produce fewer flowers.

1

Gourd, Marrow, Pumpkin
Cucurbita pepo   Cucurbitaceae

Some 25 species of this genus originate in tropical America. They
have been grown as crops for at least five thousand years.
   Cucurbita pepo is a variable gourd of creeping habit; if provided
with a support, it will climb and cling by means of tendrils. Cultivation
of ornamental gourds in the garden is no more difficult than growing
marrows.
   Ornamental gourds need a rich, well-drained soil. During their initial
growing period, they require abundant watering because their large
leaves transpire a lot of water. Occasional feeding is beneficial. If
sufficiently watered, they tolerate temperatures up to 38 °C (100 °F),
but they will not withstand frost.
   Gourds can be sown in mid-May directly into the soil, some 2.5 cm
(1 in) deep, two to three seeds at each position. They generally germinate in 10 to 14 days. To extend their period of vegetation it is advisable to sow them in March or April in pots indoors or in a propagating frame and to set out the seedlings with two pairs of leaves at the
end of May.
   Ornamental gourds are excellent subjects for quick but short-term
covering of large surfaces of beds, slopes or compost heaps. Their
large leaves, yellow flowers and fruits of fanciful shapes can also
decorate fences, walls or trellis.

The annual *Cucurbita pepo* (1) is grown
in gardens as a creeper. Its homeland is
the north of Central America and
southern North America. It forms trailing
stems up to 10 m (4 in) long.
   The fruits of ornamental gourds (2)
are characterized by a variety of shapes
resembling pears, apples, oranges,
turbans, cones, bottles. Many are
variegated or covered with bizarre
wrinkles and warts. The skin is leathery
and the pulp inedible. Well-ripened and
attractively coloured fruits can be dried in
the shade, varnished and used as winter
ornaments, for instance in a bowl or as
part of a flower arrangement. The
ripening fruits look very attractive when
hanging on a wire fence where the stems
have climbed to various heights.

2

84

1

85

Yam, Air Potato
Dioscorea bulbifera
Dioscoreaceae

The genus *Dioscorea* comprises almost 650 species of annual climbing plants; some of them are grown in the tropics and subtropics for their large edible tubers, similar to potatoes. The skin is yellow, brown or almost purple-red, but the most valued cultivars are white-skinned. All species and their cultivars have a typical heart-shaped venation on the leaves. The tiny flowers grow in axillary spikes or racemes; they are mostly dioecious. The fruit is a capsule containing two, less frequently four, seeds in each compartment.

Yams are demanding as to temperature and humidity, and can be encountered mainly in the greenhouses of the botanical gardens. Rampant species can cover entire walls. Smaller specimens, especially cultivars with multicoloured foliage, can be used as potted plants or made to climb in a heated conservatory or tropical window.

Yams are raised from tiny tubercles formed in leaf axils. In the winter months, the tubercles are stored in slightly damp peat, preferably at a temperature of 10 °C (50 °F). If grown in pots, yams can remain in them for the winter, but watering should be greatly reduced because the plants need a three-month rest period, during which the parts above the ground die off. In spring, stem cuttings with a single leaf are inserted in small pots. They take root when placed above a heating source set at 20 to 25 °C (68 to 77 °F).

Dioscorea bulbifera (1) is native to tropical Asia and the Philippines, although it is currently cultivated in tropical regions all over the world. Under favourable conditions the twining stem attains a height of 6 m (20 ft). The underground tuber is grey-white and weighs 1 to 2 kg (2 ¼ to 4 ½ lb). The tubercles (2) formed in leaf axils measure up to 15 cm (6 in). They are planted in March in a mixture of leafmould, well-rotted compost or rich loam and sand. The sprouting stems branch out and can be tied to sticks or other supports if necessary. Feeding with a balanced liquid fertilizer promotes growth of both the green parts and the tubers. If you want to achieve a better leaf colour, lower the temperature. As soon as the leaves begin to turn yellow, watering has to be reduced.

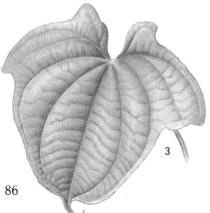

3

Dioscorea sansibarensis (3) is a native of Zaire and Madagascar. It is a vigorous species suitable for a tropical greenhouse.

2

1

Dipladenia hybrids

Apocynaceae

Tropical South America is the home of some 40 species of *Dipladenia.* They are twining shrubs or sub-shrubs, some reaching a considerable height. They are erect at first, later twine around the trunk or branches of the supporting plant.

The cultivated species include *Dipladenia sanderi* and *D. splendens* from Brazil, having flowers about 7 cm (2 ¾ in) across.

Dipladenias are relatively undemanding twining woody species suitable for cool interiors. Although they require plenty of light, partial shading is recommended at midday. Young potted plants should be tied to a support from the very beginning. Older specimens should be repotted when necessary, usually about every two to three years, young plants are repotted annually, preferably in March or April, into a peat-based potting compost.

Cuttings of ripened wood bearing a single pair of leaves are used for propagation. The cuttings are placed in lukewarm water to let the sap soak out. Then dip into hormone rooting powder and insert the cuttings into a mixture of peat and sand in a propagating frame with bottom heat. At a temperature of 22 to 25 °C (71 to 77 °F) they should put out roots in five to seven weeks. Young plants intended as pot plants must be pinched back repeatedly to promote branching. From March to August the growth is encouraged by feeding with a balanced liquid fertilizer.

It is among the hybrids of dipladenia that the most effective house plants are found. *D.* × *amoena* has deep pink flowers; *D.* × *rubiniana* (1) has ruby-red blossoms and *D.* × *rosacea* has blooms of pale pink (2). All have a yellow throat and flower generally from June to August. By providing optimum light and temperature conditions at different times of the year, flowering can be induced in March or postponed until November. This method is carried out by growers who can adjust the conditions in their greenhouses automatically. Since dipladenias form few roots, they are greatly affected by any drying out of the root ball and have to be watered regularly and with care. In winter the plants should be placed in a light position, watering reduced, and the temperature maintained at 12 to 15 °C (53 to 59 °F).

2

1

The genus *Eccremocarpus* is restricted to four species occurring in South America.

In European gardens, *Eccremocarpus scaber* is usually grown as an annual. It can be trained over walls, fences, trellis or pergolas, clinging to the support by means of leaf tendrils. If placed in a larger container, it will quickly cover a balcony wall. The tendrils can be encouraged to climb up vertically-strung plastic-covered wires. Watering and regular feeding must be provided during the vegetative period. If it is set out early and conditions are favourable, this plant attains a height of 5 m (16 ft) by autumn.

The seeds are usually sown under glass in March, and the plants germinate at 15 to 18 °C (59 to 64 °F) within two weeks. The seedlings must soon be pricked out into small pots and later potted on into larger ones. Young plants thrive in a temperature between 10 to 12 °C (50 to 53 °C). Young plants are set out in late May: they require a warm, light soil type, rich in nutrients and moisture holding.

In frost-free places the plants can survive outside throughout the winter. The plants should be cut back to some 50 cm (20 in) above the ground, covered with dry leaves or peat and plastic sheeting. Consequently, flowering takes place earlier the following year.

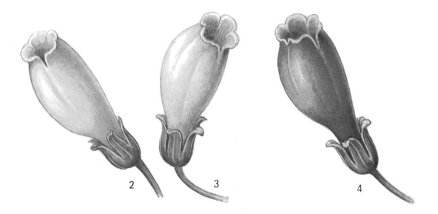

2   3   4

Eccremocarpus scaber (1) grows wild in
Chile. It is a sub-shrub reaching a height
of up to 5 m (16 ft) in its homeland, but it
is smaller by half in European conditions.
The flowers are about 2.5 cm (1 in) long
and appear in succession from June to
October. In addition to the original
red-orange species, cultivars with yellow,
pink or red blossoms are also available.
The cultivar *E. s.* 'Aureus' has
golden-yellow flowers (2); *E. s.* 'Roseus'
pink-red (3); *E. s.* 'Carmineus',
carmine-red (4), and *E. s.* 'Ruber' is dark
red. Some rare cultivars have
yellow-white-streaked foliage. This
undemanding and highly decorative
annual deserves greater popularity.

1

Flame Violet
Episcia cupreata

Gesneriaceae

The rain-forests of Central and South America are the home of over 30 species of the genus *Episcia,* herbaceous plants with creeping or trailing stems. Flowers appear from April to October but are short-lived.

As a pot plant, *Episcia cupreata* can be used only for short-term purposes because it never lasts long in the home, succeeding only in an environment with high atmospheric moisture, and a temperature of 20 to 25 °C (68 to 77 °F) in summer and 16 to 18 °C (60 to 64 °F) in winter. It does not tolerate direct sunlight.

The pendent shoots of this rather demanding plant are best displayed in hanging pots or baskets placed in a window or vitrine. In a large tropical window episcias can be used as ground-covering perennials. They can also be grown in terrariums and bottle gardens.

The plants are repotted in early spring into a peat-based potting compost. Regular winter watering is important, the amount of water being adapted to temperature and light intensity.

Episcias are easily propagated by vegetative means, and since older specimens are less handsome, it is advisable to grow new plants every year. They are obtained by cutting off young shoots which grow on the runners. Under favourable conditions in a propagating frame, kept at a temperature of about 25 °C (77 °F) it will form roots in any season.

Episcia cupreata (1), the most common species of the genus grown in pots, has its area of natural distribution in moist situations along the rivers of Colombia. The main flowering stem is only a few centimetres tall. At various intervals from the parent plant the creeping stems form thickened spots, from which baby plants with roots grow. In the wild episcias

2

1

propagate freely and soon cover a large
area. The leaves are up to 13 cm (5 in)
long and 8 cm (3 in) wide.
  The scarlet-red floral tubes are 2.5 cm
(1 in) long (2). The most common cultivar
is *Episcia cupreata* 'Silver Sheen' with
pale green leaves having a silvery-white
pattern.

Spindle Tree
Euonymus fortunei

Celastraceae

Euonymus fortunei, formerly called *E. radicans* var. *acutus*, is one of 170 species of spindle trees. Its original range of distribution is China, Japan and Korea. It is an evergreen woody plant, under favourable conditions climbing to a height of 3 m (10 ft). In modern gardening it is also used as a ground-cover plant substituting lawn on slopes or small beds. A slow grower in the first years, it later forms a dense carpet which can be cut regularly with a lawn mower set high or with shears. The young shoots are weak; unless they find a support, they creep along the ground and put out roots. The leaves are 2.5 to 5 cm (1 to 2 in) long. Umbels of tiny greenish-yellow blossoms may appear in June and July, but in Europe this species rarely produces flowers.

Euonymus flourishes in any type of garden soil containing sufficient moisture. It also succeeds in semi-shade, although it gives better foliage colour in the sun. It withstands heavy pruning, which is an important quality when the plant is used for ground cover. Older climbing plants are cut back from time to time to encourage new growths from below.

Euonymus fortunei can be easily increased by division of rooted shoots. Gardeners use mainly cuttings taken either in late winter or in August. The cuttings, 5 to 8 cm (2 to 3 in) long, form roots in a mixture of peat and sand within a few weeks.

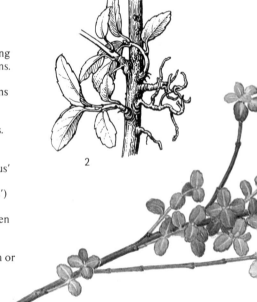

Euonymus fortunei (1) is a creeping plant, easily taking root, rarely flowering and bearing fruit in European conditions. It has dull green leaves with pale veins and a reddish sheen in winter. The stems (2) tend to root readily as soon as they touch the ground, or cling to a support and climb to a height of several metres.

There are many cultivars including *E. fortunei* 'Carrieri' with glossy green leaves, up to 5 cm (2 in) long, 'Coloratus' with deep purple autumn and winter foliage, and 'Variegatus' (syn. 'Gracilis') producing leaves marked with yellow-white (3) which are pinkish when sprouting and in winter. *E. fortunei* 'Kewensis' (4) has thin twigs with tiny leaves and is suitable for a rock garden or for covering low walls.

3

1

4

Russian Vine
Polygonum baldschuanicum

Polygonaceae

The genus *Polygonum* has recently been divided up. The annuals and herbaceous plants form the genus *Polygonum* and the vigorous, deciduous, twining, woody plants now form the genus *Fallopia*. But as the new name is not yet in common usage we will refer to the plants under the original name to avoid confusion. Polygonums do well in any type of ordinary garden soil and withstand polluted atmospheres. They tolerate shady situations but will flower more profusely in full sun.

Polygonum baldschuanicum is an undemanding plant and its lush greenery soon covers a large area. It is often used to mask unsightly wire fences; it grows through the netting and forms an impenetrable screen. It can be clipped over with shears to prevent it from invading the neighbouring garden. If planted against a pergola, the weight of the adult plant has to be anticipated when planning the size of the pergola and choosing construction materials.

P. baldschuanicum is propagated by hardwood cuttings taken from one-year-old shoots before the first frosts. In January the cuttings are inserted in pots filled with well-drained, nutrient-rich soil and placed in a cold house.

To restrict their invasive habit, the plants have to be cut hard back from time to time. The new shoots flower even more profusely. Severe frosts can damage the plants, but they usually shoot again the following year.

Polygonum baldschuanicum (1) may still be found under the name of *Bilderdykia baldschuanica*, even in recent publications. It is native to Tadzhikistan in the U.S.S.R., occurring at heights of around 1,500 to 2,000 m (4,920 to 6,560 ft). Even in the European climate it often reaches a height of 15 m (50 ft). The leaves are up to 10 cm (33 ft) long. The white blossoms (2) are about 5 mm (1/4 in) across and at the end of flowering develop a pinkish sheen and turn a deeper colour below. The flowers are fragrant and frequently visited by bees. They are arranged in very long and loosely branched panicles. *P. baldschuanicum* flowers from July to October. Seeds are rarely formed.

1

2

Creeping Fig
Ficus pumila
Moraceae

The genus *Ficus* comprises some 2,000 species of woody plants, many attaining the size of robust trees. The climbing species grown in the home include *Ficus pumila*, sometimes called *F. stipulata*, a native of Japan, China and Australia. This evergreen climber reaches a height of 80 cm (32 in). Some rarer, slow-growing cultivars are also available: *F. pumila* 'Minima' with leaves about 1 cm (¹/₂ in) long, and *F. pumila* 'Variegata' with white-spotted foliage.

Ficus sagittata, also known uder the name of *F. radicans*, is found from the eastern Himalayas to the Philippines and Micronesia. The leaves are up to 6 cm (2 ¹/₄ in) long and evergreen. The cultivar 'Variegata' has white-spotted leaves, requires a warmer environment and grows more slowly.

Both species are cultivated as house plants only in their juvenile state. They enjoy high temperatures and adapt well to fluctuations of light. Drying up of the root ball usually causes the leaves to drop. A diluted dose of a compound fertilizer can be given no more than two or three times during the main growing period.

Both these ficus species are easily propagated from cuttings. Softwood cuttings are inserted in suitably sized pots in a propagating frame with bottom heat. If a humid atmosphere is maintained and the cuttings are watered regularly, they should take root within four weeks.

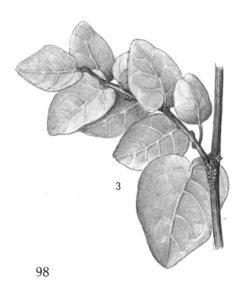

3

Ficus pumila (1) is a creeping plant with tiny, relatively thin leaves, about 2.5 cm (1 in) long. Adventitious roots (3, 4) are formed on the weak stems on the side away from the light. The plant uses these roots to cling to smooth surfaces.
  Young plants are suitable for both cool and warm interiors, although the best results are achieved in a closed humid environment where the plants can climb over a branch. Gardeners often put *F. pumila* in bowls or pots and train it up a moss-covered stick (2). In frost-free, mild regions it can be left outside in a garden under a light cover throughout the winter, without suffering any damage.

1

2

4

Fuchsia
Fuchsia × hybrida   Onagraceae

About 100 species of fuchsia are known so far. They all originate in Central and South America, where they occur in humid mountain forests up to a height of 3,000 m (9,850 ft). They are sub-shrubs, shrubs or trees with many branches, usually pendent. They bear flowers from May to October without interruption; in a greenhouse they will flower almost all year long.

Fuchsia × hybrida tolerates a shady situation, therefore ranking among the plants which in summer can be used in window boxes or containers with a northerly or north-easterly aspect but getting some morning sun. They do well in a humid environment, in the vicinity of water. Fuchsias are at their loveliest in rainy summer. If regular and copious watering is provided, they can be placed in the sun with success. The soil should be rich in humus and nutrients, with a pH of 6.0.

Half-hardy fuchsias have to be hardened off before being put out in late May. Until mid-August, they should be fed once a week. Half-hardy fuchsias have to be moved indoors before the first frosts. The best winter temperatures are 3 to 5 °C (37 to 41 °F); watering has to be restricted and the plants given plenty of light. In March they are cut back to about 15 cm (6 in) above the ground, repotted and allowed to sprout.

Propagation is by softwood cuttings with three pairs of leaves, without flowers or flower buds if possible. The best time for propagation is between May and August.

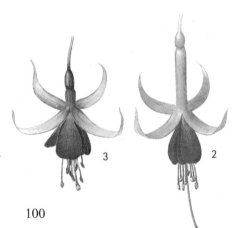

3   2

The common name of *Fuchsia × hybrida* covers cultivars resulting from cross-breeding of *F. magellanica, F. coccinea, F. arborescens, F. corymbiflora* and others. The individual cultivars have smaller or bigger flowers, single or double, white, pink, red and purple, often with petals and sepals of different hues. Many are of pendent habit and therefore suitable for window or balcony boxes, hanging baskets or large flower bowls.

Some good cultivars include *Fuchsia × hybrida* 'Márinka' with single to semi-double flowers, red sepals and

purple-blue petals (1); 'Mr W. Rundle'
with single, pink-orange flowers (2);
'Cara Mia', semi-double, white-pink with
purple-red corolla (3), and 'Gypsy
Queen', double, with purple-violet
petals (4).

101

Glory Lily
Gloriosa rothschildiana
Liliaceae

The genus *Gloriosa* includes only 6 species found in periodically drought-ridden areas of tropical Africa and Asia.

Gloriosa rothschildiana from Uganda is the best-known species. It has an underground tuberous rootstock and is cultivated in greenhouses for its exotic flowers. The plants attach themselves by tendrils to wire nets, up to 2 m (6 ft) high.

Gloriosas grown in greenhouses or indoors need an optimum temperature of about 20 °C (68 °F) in their growing period. They require light in winter and semi-shade in summer.

In early March, the tuberous rootstock is placed some 5 cm (2 in) deep in a large pot. As soon as it has sprouted, the shoot is tied to a support about 1 m (3 ft) tall. During one growing season the plant will produce approximately as many flowers as the rootstock measures in centimetres. After flowering the rootstock ripens in dry soil for six to eight weeks. It is then stored in dry peat or sand in a place with a temperature of 17 °C (62 °F) and atmospheric humidity of 70 per cent.

The plants can be raised from seeds sown in a bowl or box filled with leafmould, peat and sand. At a temperature of 20 to 22 °C (68 to 71 °F) they germinate within 60 days. They can be potted or planted in a garden bed only in the mildest and most protected areas of the country. The flowers are usually produced the third year.

Gloriosa rothschildiana (1) grows up to 2 m (6 ft) tall, with twining, much-branched stems. The leaves measure 13 cm (5 in), their tips are elongated into tendrils which cling to a support. The exotic-looking flowers are 13 cm (5 in) across. The natural flowering period is June and July, but it can be altered by shifting the time of planting and achieving two flowering periods a year in a greenhouse.

The elongated capsule (2) contains some 90 seeds which turn black on ripening. The underground tuberous rootstocks have a yellow-white skin, they are 2.5 cm (1 in) wide and up to 25 cm (10 in) long. The cultivar 'Citrina' has lemon-yellow blossoms with a mauve pattern.

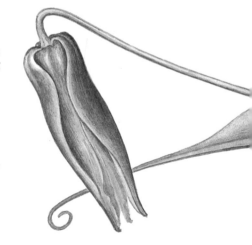

1

2

103

Gynura scandens

Compositae

The genus *Gynura* comprises 24 species of perennials or sub-shrubs distributed mainly in warm regions of Asia and Africa. Their most attractive features are the unusual foliage tints. The flowerheads are composed of up to 20 florets and give off an unpleasant smell.

Gynura scandens was introduced as a house plant after World War II. It can attain a considerable height within a few years if grown in a greenhouse. It needs a support, preferably a strong wire, but it is often cultivated as trailing plant in a suspended container.

Gynuras require plenty of light to develop the colour of their foliage. The best temperatures are 20 to 22 °C (68 to 71 °F) in summer and 15 °C (59 °F) in winter. They tolerate the dry air in centrally-heated homes and can be placed outside in summer because they withstand high temperatures.

During the growing period watering must be abundant, but to avoid unsightly spots the leaves must never be sprayed. The plants have to be pinched back repeatedly to encourage branching, as older leaves lose their decorative tints. Cuttings take root in water or in a lime-free mixture of peat and sand. Three to five rooted cuttings can be planted in a pot.

1

104

Gynura scandens (1) is a sub-shrub from tropical eastern Africa. The leaves are smaller than in *G. aurantiaca* and the flowers are orange, produced from April to September. It is a trailing house plant.

Gynura aurantiaca (3) is a sub-shrub native to the mountain forests of Java. The leaves are elongated, up to 20 cm (8 in) long. The flowerheads are orange-yellow in colour and appear from September to October, although they can also appear at other times. They flower in succesion and do not open out like other species of the Compositae. The colour of petals soon turns a silver-white (2). The seeds with their feathery appendages are not used for propagation because both species are easily raised from cuttings.

2

3

Persian Ivy
Hedera colchica
Araliaceae

The genus *Hedera* comprises only 7 species found in Europe, Asia and northern Africa. They are evergreen climbing plants holding fast to a support by means of aerial roots growing in groups on the undersides of sterile stems. The fruiting stems are more branched and erect, and they do not form these adventitious roots. Only older and larger specimens produce the semi-spherical umbels of yellow-green blossoms. The fruits ripen in the spring of the following year.

Ivies are ornamental plants for cool interiors. Green-leaved cultivars succeed in a winter temperature of 10 to 16 °C (50 to 60 °F), cultivars with variegated foliage do best in winter at 16 to 18 °C (60 to 64 °F). Although ivies can be kept in the home throughout the year, they benefit from spending the summer in a shady site in the open. House plants should be taken inside before the first autumn frost although the Persian Ivy can be grown outside in a sheltered spot in the garden during the winter.

Watering must be regular and adapted to seasonal requirements. Young plants are repotted annually, older specimens once every two to four years, in a soil-based compost.

In the home ivies can be placed in pots or in bowls with other plants, and in various suspended containers. They can be trained over trellis or dividing screens.

Hedera colchica (1) is native to the Caucasus and northern Iran. Only the juvenile plant is grown as a house plant. This has large heart-shaped leaves with entire margins, up to 20 cm (8 in) long and 15 cm (6 in) wide. The flowering shoots of mature adult plants bear smaller leaves (2).

The varieties and cultivars with variegated foliage are more demanding as to warmth and light, but they should not be placed in direct sunshine. The cultivar *H. colchica* 'Dentata Aurea' has yellow-marbled leaves (3) and 'Dentata Variegata' produces leaves with white and yellow rims. These cultivars can be increased only by vegetative means, usually by cuttings.

1

3

2

Common Ivy
Hedera helix

Araliaceae

The Common Ivy is distributed in most of Europe and Asia. Under favourable conditions it reaches a height of 12 to 20 m (40 to 65 ft). In juvenile state it forms lobed leaves, 4 to 13 cm (1 ½ to 5 in) long. The leaves on fruiting branches have an entire margin and measure up to 14 cm (5 ½ in).

In addition to the species, cultivars are available, differing in the shape and coloration of the leaves or in size. For instance *Hedera helix* 'Arborescens' is a fertile, flowering and fruiting form of the original species, propagated by vegetative means and forming a rounded, profusely flowering shrub, up to 2 m (6 ft) high. *H. helix* 'Sagittifolia' has smaller five-lobed leaves with the central lobe the largest and triangular in shape; *H. helix* 'Conglomerata' is low-growing, with small, dark green leaves with fewer lobes. Providing the cultivars grow in sufficiently nourishing and moist soil, they tolerate a city or roadside environment.

Propagation is by means of cuttings, which can be placed in pots or garden beds any time in spring or summer.

The frost-resistant species and many of the cultivars are suitable for the garden. They are planted against a rough-surfaced wall or fence to which they can cling easily, or against the trunk of a large tree with coarse bark or old tree stump, on which they climb up to the crown.

Cultivars of *Hedera helix* are grown as favourite pot plants, but exclusively in their juvenile state. *H. helix* 'Sagittifolia' (1) is recommended for its attractively shaped, narrow-lobed leaves.

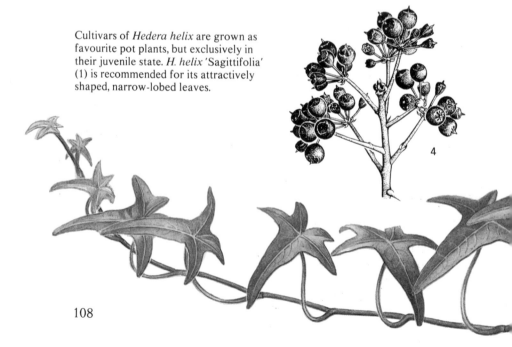

4

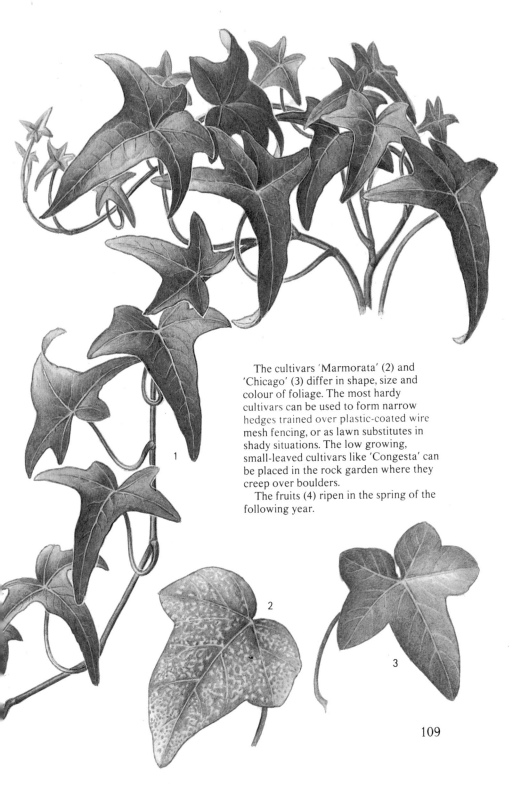

The cultivars 'Marmorata' (2) and 'Chicago' (3) differ in shape, size and colour of foliage. The most hardy cultivars can be used to form narrow hedges trained over plastic-coated wire mesh fencing, or as lawn substitutes in shady situations. The low growing, small-leaved cultivars like 'Congesta' can be placed in the rock garden where they creep over boulders.

The fruits (4) ripen in the spring of the following year.

1

2

3

Miniature Wax Plant
Hoya bella   Asclepiadaceae

Over 100 species of *Hoya* are native to south-eastern Asia and Australia. They are woody climbing or creeping plants with evergreen, leathery leaves. The strong-scented flowers appear from May to September.

Hoya bella is more demanding in terms of conditions and cultivation than the more frequently grown *H. carnosa*. To display the trailing branches to best advantage the plants are placed in suspended containers or grown over a piece of branch wood.

This warmth-loving species requires an optimum summer temperature of 25 °C (77 °F) and a winter temperature of 18 °C (64 °F). The plants develop better shoots and produce more flowers in a well lit position, sheltered from scorching sunshine.

During the growth and flowering period, the plants need ample watering and a fortnightly feed of a liquid fertilizer with low nitrogen content. Wax flowers should not be moved or turned around without reason, as they respond by dropping their buds. Older specimens are transplanted once every two to four years, preferably in spring. To encourage the formation of flower buds, a minimum six-week period of relative rest with reduced watering is required, terminating in late February.

Hoya bella is a weak grower on its own roots, and it should be grafted on a well-rooted stock of *H. carnosa*. The best time for grafting is spring, just before the new growth begins. The plants are left in a propagating frame for two to three weeks to allow scion and stock to become united.

2

Hoya bella (1) is native to India. It is a much-branched plant of trailing habit. The leaves are succulent, about 2.5 cm (1 in) long. The blossoms (2) are only 1 cm ($^1/_2$ in) wide, arranged in umbels composed of eight to twelve flowers. They look as if made of wax or milk glass and give off a pleasant scent. For reasons yet unknown, some clones produce flowers in the juvenile state, while others take years to bloom. The withered inflorescences must not be removed because new flowers grow from them the following year.

1

Wax Flower, Porcelain Flower
Hoya carnosa
Asclepiadaceae

Hoya carnosa is a favourite house plant. Providing the leaves are occasionally mist-sprayed and the dust washed away, it tolerates even a dusty environment. It is an excellent subject for training over decorative trellis and older plants easily cover a large wall. This plant can also be grown hydroponically.

Hoya carnosa is less particular than *H. bella* and does well in a winter temperature between 12 to 15 °C (53 to 59 °F). It withstands the dry air of centrally-heated homes. In the summer months, potted plants can be plunged in the ground in a suitable place in the garden.

Softwood or stem cuttings from well-ripened shoots are used for propagation, preferably in spring, or under favourable conditions in any season. Cuttings with one or two pairs of leaves are inserted in small pots filled with a mixture of peat and sand and placed in a propagating frame. They usually take root within four to five weeks, at a temperature of about 22 °C (71 °F) if supplied with adequate light and moisture. They are potted on into larger pots and trained up sticks or over cane arches. The plants grown from cuttings usually flower for the first time in their second or third year.

Regular watering is important in the growing and flowering season. In January and February, excessive watering can cause a disease of the roots and consequent leaf drop, so cut down on watering in winter. Older plants are repotted in spring, once every two to four years, into a soil-based potting compost.

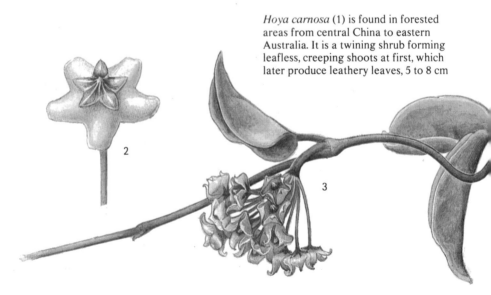

Hoya carnosa (1) is found in forested areas from central China to eastern Australia. It is a twining shrub forming leafless, creeping shoots at first, which later produce leathery leaves, 5 to 8 cm

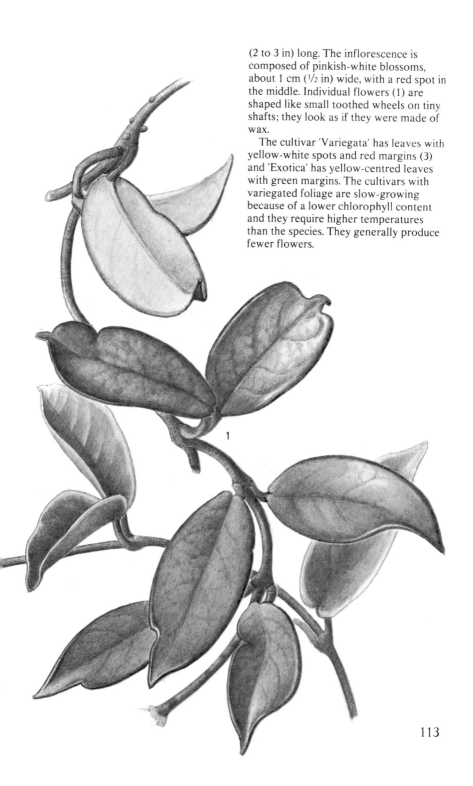

(2 to 3 in) long. The inflorescence is
composed of pinkish-white blossoms,
about 1 cm (½ in) wide, with a red spot in
the middle. Individual flowers (1) are
shaped like small toothed wheels on tiny
shafts; they look as if they were made of
wax.

The cultivar 'Variegata' has leaves with
yellow-white spots and red margins (3)
and 'Exotica' has yellow-centred leaves
with green margins. The cultivars with
variegated foliage are slow-growing
because of a lower chlorophyll content
and they require higher temperatures
than the species. They generally produce
fewer flowers.

1

Climbing Hydrangea
Hydrangea petiolaris
Saxifragaceae

The genus *Hydrangea* contains some 35 species out of which two are of climbing habit.

Hydrangea petiolaris, also listed as *H. scandens,* is not common in the gardens of Europe and Britain, although older plants withstand harsh winters without ill effects. This climbing species needs a sheltered and slightly shaded site. The soil should be rich in humus and nutrients, slightly acid and quite moist.

In a favourable location, the plants can be long lived and cover a large area. They are best suited for covering a north-facing wall of a house. They can also climb up the trunk of a large tree to the crown.

Hydrangeas are planted out with root balls, preferably in spring, so as to be able to form roots before winter. Soft water must be used for watering and the root ball must never be allowed to dry out. A compound fertilizer can be applied in the growing season. Occasional pruning is sufficient to give the new growths space.

Propagation is mainly by layering. In spring, one-year-old shoots are placed in shallow ridges and covered, with their tips sticking out. The rooted parts are separated the following year and transplanted to their permanent site.

Hydrangea petiolaris is native to the woods of Japan, Korea, central China and Taiwan. It grows to a height of 10 to 20 m (33 to 66 ft) in its homeland; in Europe it reaches a maximum height of about 5 m (16 ft). The adventitious roots (3) grow along the length of pale brown stems

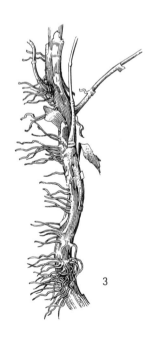

3

2

114

enabling them to cling to the support.
The root-bearing stems do not produce
flowers.
 The leaves are up to 15 cm (6 in) long.
The inflorescence (1) is between 20 and
25 cm (8 and 10 in) across. It is a flat

umbel composed of tiny fertile flowers
surrounded by a ring of white sterile
flowers, up to 2.5 cm (1 in) across (2). The
flowering period is generally in June and
July. The leaves are often entirely
covered by a mass of blossoms

Morning Glory
Ipomoea tricolor
Convolvulaceae

The nomenclature of the genus *Ipomoea* is very confused, because some species listed under the genera *Pharbitis* and *Quamoclit* are included by some experts in this genus.

Ipomoea tricolor, synonymous with *Pharbitis rubrocaerulea* and *P. tricolor,* is the most common garden species. In Mexico, its homeland, it has been grown as a garden plant for centuries. It is a perennial in its natural habitat, but in European conditions it is sown every year as an annual. The plants may mask a wire fence or cover a balcony, loggia or garden terrace. Morning glories are planted in large containers placed near a construction up which the plants can climb. They thrive against walls with a southerly exposure, using a support of trellis, strung wires or strings but they never form a dense or opaque screen. Their beauty is very short-lived, terminated by the first autumn frost.

Morning Glories like a sheltered, warm and sunny site. The soil should be deep, rich in humus and slightly alkaline.

They are sown in late March or early April in small pots placed under glass. Seeds germinate within five to fourteen days. Young plants are tied to sticks at first but later climb on their own.

Ipomoea tricolor (1) reaches a height of 3 m (10 ft) and its flowers are 8 to 10 cm (3 to 4 in) wide. The edges of the petals are red-tinged when the flowers open, and later change to azure-blue. Flowering generally takes place in August and September. A number of cultivars have been bred, such as *I. tricolor* 'Blaustern' with blue flowers and a dark star, or 'Crimson Rambler' with carmine blossoms. In the cultivar 'Darling' the throat is white and the edge carmine-red, and 'Heavenly Blue' has azure-blue flowers which appear very early and later turn purple-red.

2

Pharbitis purpurea (2) is another annual from tropical America. It attains a height of up to 3 m (10 ft). The flowers, up to 6 cm (2¼ in) across, appear in July and August. Its requirements as to environment, cultivation, use and propagation are similar to those of Morning Glory.

1

Winter Jasmine
Jasminum nudiflorum   Oleaceae

About 200 species of this genus are found in the tropics and sub-tropics of the Northern Hemisphere.

The Winter Jasmine is the only frost-resistant species, bearing flowers in winter. The blossoms occur along the entire length of branches. They withstand low winter temperatures and long-lasting frosts. The flowers are borne on old wood and any unnecessary pruning should therefore be avoided. The soil must be deep, humus-rich and not too dry.

The plants need plenty of rain before the onset of winter, because their deep green, bare branches transpire throughout the winter months. The old shoots should be occasionally pruned back to the ground, forcing the shrub to form new shoots which will bear masses of flowers the following year.

The Winter Jasmine is easily propagated by layering, since its branches touch the ground and put out roots freely; they can be separated from the parent plant the following year and transplanted to their permanent site. Stem cuttings can be taken from May to July, inserted in boxes under glass. Cuttings of well-ripened wood can be struck in winter, placed in pots and kept in a greenhouse.

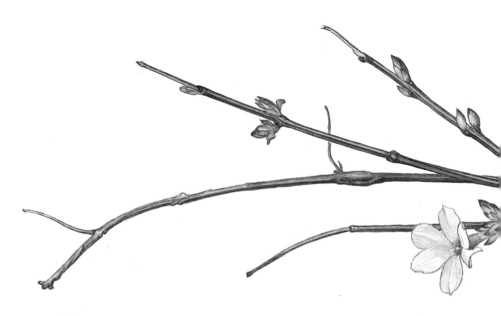

Jasminum nudiflorum (1) is native to
western China. It is a deciduous shrub
with arching branches, up to 2 m (10 ft)
long. The flowers are formed on old
wood before the leaves appear, from
December to April depending on the site.
The first blooms are often covered by
snow or frost and the flowering continues
into spring. The blossoms are about 1 cm
(¹/₂ in) across and sweetly scented.

   The leaves (2) are about 2.5 cm (1 in)
long and appear in April. The plants
thrive against a north-facing wall, but
they flower earlier in a sunny position.
They are tied to a trellis or training wires.
They are attractive subjects for archways
or dry walls where the branches hang
down the slope. The branches cut in
winter will flower readily indoors.

2

1

Sweet Pea
Lathyrus odoratus
Leguminosae

Some 100 species of pea are distributed in the temperate zone of the Northern Hemisphere and in South America. They are climbing annuals or perennials forming leaf tendrils which cling to any support.

The most common garden pea, *Lathyrus odoratus,* is a native of southern Italy and Sicily. It is used for training over a wire fence, balcony wall or in window boxes. Sweet Peas produce masses of fine, pastel-coloured flowers which last in the vase for several days. The regular cutting of the flowers makes the plant bloom longer. If the blossoms are allowed to wither on the plant, seeds form in pods and the above-ground parts of the plant soon wither.

Sweet Peas do well in a warm and sunny site with deep, well-drained rich soil. They are lime-loving.

Young plants tolerate low temperatures and can be sown directly into the open in mid-April, two or three seeds to a station, about 5 cm (2 in) deep. Seeds remain capable of germination for about three years. At a temperature between 15 to 18 °C (59 to 64 °F) they sprout within a fortnight.

When the roots become too dry, the leaves begin to drop; therefore regular watering is important in periods of drought. During the flowering period Sweet Peas should be fed every two weeks.

Lathyrus odoratus (1) is a commonly cultivated climbing annual holding to its support by means of leaf tendrils. It attains a height of 1 to 2.5 m (3 to 8 ft). The species has pink blossoms with a pleasant scent. A number of cultivars have been bred from the species, differing in size, flowering season and colour of blossoms and it is these that are most often grown. The best cultivars include 'Pink Pride' (2), carmine-pink with a white centre; 'Danny' (3), dark blue; 'White Ensign' (4), pure white, and many others. All flower generally from June to August, but the season can be adjusted according to the time of sowing. Sweet Peas can be grown under glass to produce crop over a longer season. The fruit is a slender, hairy legume (5).

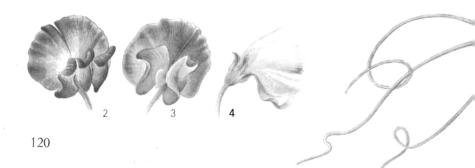

2   3   4

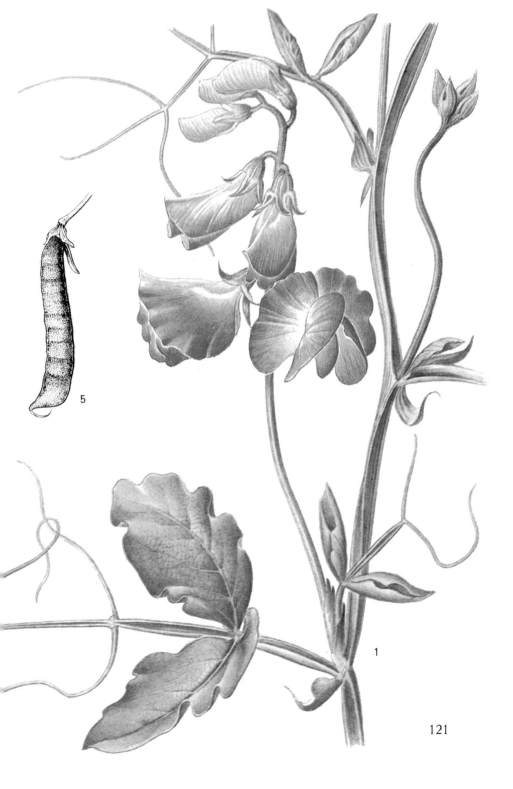

5

1

121

Perfoliate Honeysuckle
Lonicera caprifolium
Caprifoliaceae

The genus *Lonicera* comprises some 180 species found predominantly in the temperate and subtropical zones of the Northern Hemisphere. They include deciduous and evergreen species. Only a small number of species have a twining habit.

The Perfoliate Honeysuckle is a climbing woody plant, excellent for covering fences, walls or trellis, columns, garden gates and pergolas. If left without support, it behaves like a creeper and soon spreads over a large area. The twining shoots grow by 50 cm (20 in) every year. Older plants become bare in the lower parts, so heavy pruning has to be carried out every few years.

This comparatively undemanding, frost-resistant species withstands both sun and semi-shade. It prefers open moist soil, rich in nutrients.

Cultivars include the common 'Alba' flowering in the first half of May, with lighter leaves and blooms of white. 'Pauciflora' has the outside of the flower tube coloured a deeper red than in the species.

The Perfoliate Honeysuckle is propagated by stratified seeds in spring. The cultivars can be increased only by vegetative means: layering, hardwood and softwood cuttings.

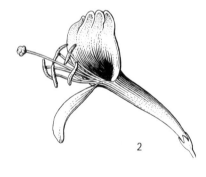

2

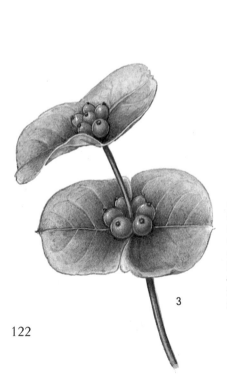

Lonicera caprifolium (1) is a European species occurring on scrub-covered slopes and in moist soil at the margins of woods. It is deciduous and climbs in a clockwise direction up to 5 m (16 ft) high. The tubular flowers (2) are about 4.5 cm (1 ¾ in) long and emit a pleasant fragrance, especially in the evening. That is the reason why the shrub is visited by

3

1

moths, attracted by the scent and the showy shades of the flowers.

After flowering, red berries are formed in leaf axils, grouped around the stem (3). The berries measure about 5 mm (¼ in) across and ripen in September. They usually do not last long because they are consumed by birds in winter.

Honeysuckle
Lonicera japonica
Caprifoliaceae

Lonicera japonica is found in the wild in Japan, China and Taiwan, growing to a height of 6 m (20 ft). It was first brought to Britain in 1806. This clockwise twining woody species has leaves up to 5 cm (2 in) long and 2.5 cm (1 in) wide which are evergreen in most conditions. The flowers are about 4 cm (1 ½ in) long, yellow-white with a red flush when opening, yellow at the end of flowering. They emit a pleasant scent. Flowering takes place in June and July. Propagation is by hardwood cuttings or by layering of one-year-old shoots. This species prefers open moist soil.

Lonicera giraldii comes from north-western China. It is an evergreen climber, reaching a height of 2 m (6 ft). The leaves measure 4 to 9 cm (1 ½ to 3 ½ in) and they are covered with soft yellow hairs. The flowers are only 2 cm (¾ in) long, purple-red in colour and appear in June and July.

Lonicera henryi occurs in western China and attains a height of 3 to 4 m (10 to 13 ft). It is a vigorous evergreen climber which produces lovely yellow-red blossoms in early summer.

Lonicera sempervirens, the Trumpet Honeysuckle, is native to the south-eastern United States. It is a loosely twining species retaining most of its leaves in winter. The flowers are about 4.5 cm (1 ¾ in) long, orange-red and scentless.

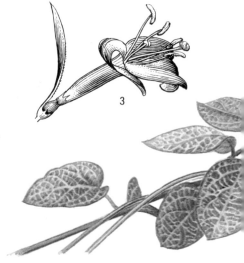

Many cultivars and varieties of *Lonicera japonica* are grown in gardens. Very popular is the cultivar 'Aureoreticulata' (1) with shoots attaining a length of 2 m (6 ft), leaves with a marked yellow-white venation and yellow-white flowers. It can be damaged by frost but will shoot again in spring. It does well in the light shade of shrubs or a wall which give some protection during winter. *L. j. halliana* has blossoms white to begin with, later turning yellow. *L. j. repens,* sometimes referred to as *L. flexuosa,* has weak trailing stems and fragrant red flowers.

Lonicera henryi (2) is an evergreen or semi-evergreen species with leaves up to 7 cm (2 ¾ in) long. The blossoms (3), measuring about 2 cm (¾ in), open in June and July.

125

Woodbine
Lonicera periclymenum
Caprifoliaceae

Lonicera periclymenum is found in the wild in clearings in moist woodlands throughout Europe, northern Africa and Asia Minor. Its strong stems climb up to the light through the trunks and branches of other woody species; Woodbine is capable of strangling its supporting plants. It is a multi-purpose plant for parks and gardens. It is undemanding but prefers moist soil. Propagation is by softwood or hardwood cuttings.

In its homeland, western China, *Lonicera alseuosmoides* reaches a height of 3 to 5 m (10 to 16 ft). The leaves are 2.5 to 6 cm (1 to 2¼ in) long and evergreen. The flowers are purple-yellow and only 1 cm (½ in) long. They appear from July to September and are followed by black, downy berries.

Lonicera etrusca is native to the Mediterranean. It is a deciduous or semi-deciduous species, retaining or shedding its leaves according to how mild or harsh the winter is. It is best planted in a warm, sunny sheltered site. The flowers are yellow-red, 4 cm (1½ in) long and sweetly scented. They open in June, July and August.

Lonicera hirsuta is a North American deciduous species. It grows to a height of 4 m (13 ft). The flowers are orange-yellow, about 2.5 cm (1 in) long and appear in June and July. *L. hirsuta* is quite hardy. The leaves are oval, elongated and pointed, with a marked net-like venation and grey-green beneath.

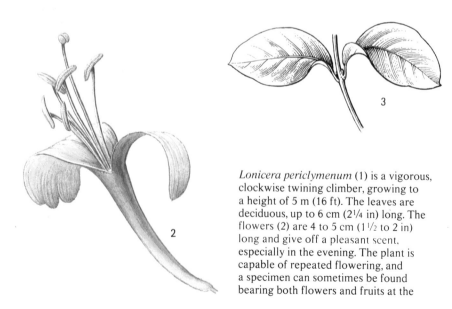

Lonicera periclymenum (1) is a vigorous, clockwise twining climber, growing to a height of 5 m (16 ft). The leaves are deciduous, up to 6 cm (2¼ in) long. The flowers (2) are 4 to 5 cm (1½ to 2 in) long and give off a pleasant scent, especially in the evening. The plant is capable of repeated flowering, and a specimen can sometimes be found bearing both flowers and fruits at the

1

same time. Unlike *L. caprifolium*, the
leaves, including the uppermost pairs,
are not fused (3).

Less vigorous cultivars are better
suited to gardens. 'Belgica', the Early
Dutch Honeysuckle, has purple-red
flowers fading to yellow and appearing in
May and June. 'Serotina', the Late Dutch
Honeysuckle, has purple-red flowers
which appear in August and September.

Scarlet Trumpet Honeysuckle
Lonicera × brownii

Caprifoliaceae

Lonicera × brownii, a 2 to 3 m (6 to 10 ft) high shrub, is a result of crossing of two North American species, *L. hirsuta* and *L. sempervirens*, in the middle of the 19th century. It is hardier than either of its parents. The stems wind in loose coils around a supporting construction or cling to the branches of surrounding shrubs or trees. The leaves are about 7 cm (2 ¾ in) long and deciduous. *L. × brownii* has yielded many cultivars. *L. × brownii* 'Fuchsioides' is a semi-evergreen cultivar about 3 m (10 ft) high. Its scarlet-red, narrow flower tubes resemble fuchsia flowers and measure 2.5 to 4 cm (1 to 1 ½ in). *L. × brownii* 'Plantierensis' is a more vigorous cultivar with larger, coral-red blossoms appearing in the same months as the species, May to August. *L. × brownii* 'Punicea' is slow-growing and has carmine-red flowers flushed orange.

Most cultivated species and cultivars tolerate both sunny and shady sites. The soil above the roots, in particular, should be shaded from the hot midday sun by surrounding plants or stone slabs. Honeysuckles succeed in light, sandy soils as well as in heavier clays. They thrive in neutral soils but also do well in acid or heavily alkaline soil. Since their root system is shallow, the soil must be moist and rich in humus and nutrients.

2

Lonicera × brownii 'Dropmore Scarlet Trumpet' (1) is a Canadian cultivar, relatively frost-resistant. The leaves remain on the shrub for a long time. The flowering season lasts from June to October; the fiery red scentless flowers, 2.5 to 4 cm (1 to 1 ½ in) long, arranged in whorls, open successively. They are followed by the fruits, two- to four-seeded berries (2), which ripen from September to November. *L. × brownii* and its cultivars are characterized by narrow tube-like flowers with very short margins (3). The flowers have two lips and are slightly convex at the base. This honeysuckle is an excellent subject to cover fences, walls, columns, small pergolas and dividing walls. The flowers can be used in flower arrangements, but they are short-lived when cut.

1

3

Honeysuckle
Lonicera × heckrottii

Caprifoliaceae

Lonicera × heckrottii is a cross between *L. × americana* and *L. sempervirens*, produced at the end of 19th century. It is commonly planted in parks and gardens but it needs nutrient-rich soil. It is also used as a fast-growing cover for fences, dilapidated walls or unsightly sheds. It deserves a more widespread distribution.

Despite its scientific name, *Lonicera × americana* does not originate in America; it is a hybrid of two European species, *L. caprifolium* and *L. etrusca*. It grows wild in the south of France, reaching a height of 6 m (20 ft). Only half of this size can be attained in the central European conditions.

The inter-species honeysuckle hybrids and their cultivars can be propagated only by vegetative means. The best method is to layer two-year-old shoots on shallow ridges and cover them with soil. The rooted parts can be separated the following year and transferred to the permanent site.

Less vigorous species such as *L. × brownii, L. × heckrottii* and their cultivars can be raised from well-ripened hardwood cuttings taken in early winter and inserted in greenhouse beds or in pots, which can be stood outside from April onwards.

Lonicera × heckrottii (1) is a slightly twining shrub, about 3 m (10 ft) tall. It bears a profusion of flowers arranged in dense whorls, from June to August. The tubular flowers are some 4 cm (1½ in) long, vividly coloured and strongly scented. The cultivar 'Gold Flame' has yellow-throated, red-orange flowers.

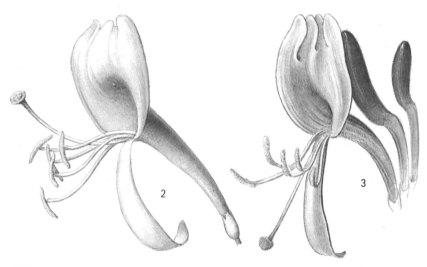

2

3

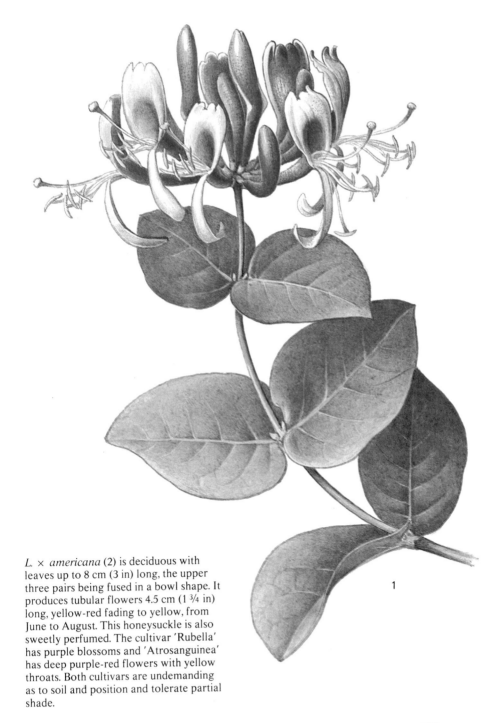

L. × *americana* (2) is deciduous with leaves up to 8 cm (3 in) long, the upper three pairs being fused in a bowl shape. It produces tubular flowers 4.5 cm (1 ¾ in) long, yellow-red fading to yellow, from June to August. This honeysuckle is also sweetly perfumed. The cultivar 'Rubella' has purple blossoms and 'Atrosanguinea' has deep purple-red flowers with yellow throats. Both cultivars are undemanding as to soil and position and tolerate partial shade.

1

131

Honeysuckle
Lonicera × tellmanniana
Caprifoliaceae

Lonicera × tellmanniana is another inter-species hybrid, crossed in Hungary in 1920 from the North American *L. sempervirens* and the Chinese species *L. tragophylla*. The hybrid has surpassed the good qualities of both parents — vigorous growth, colour of flowers and hardiness. The only shortcoming is the lack of fragrance. This honeysuckle is more demanding than the previous species and cultivars. It requires heavier and nutrient-rich soil in a site sheltered from winter sun and wind. It needs plenty of light, but scorching sunshine must never warm up the soil above the roots. The roots can be protected by planting low-growing shrubs and perennials in the surroundings.

Most honeysuckles reach a maximum height of 3 to 4 m (10 to 13 ft) and this influences their use in the garden. They are usually planted against fences, trellis, garden gates, columns and walls. Only the most vigorous species can be trained over pergolas or larger constructions. They need a solid support and the shoots should be tied in until they are able to twine themselves properly.

Water is important during the growing season. The general health and flowering of the plant is promoted by an occasional feed in spring and summer, but never after mid-August as the new growths must be allowed to mature before the onset of winter.

Lonicera × tellmanniana (1) is a relatively fast-growing, stem-twining woody plant up to 5 m (16 ft) high. The leaves are about 8 cm (3 in) long and 4 cm (1 ½ in) wide. The uppermost pair is fused in a bowl shape, the others are separated. The beautiful tubular flowers are about 4.5 cm (1 ¾ in) long (2). They open in successsion from late May to early July.

1

Climbing honeysuckles tend to
become bare in their lower parts, so
should be cut back in early spring to
about 50 cm (20 in) above the ground, or
other young plants of the same species or
cultivar should be planted in front of them
to cover the bare spots. A successful
scheme is to plant Winter Jasmine in
front of honeysuckles; it fills in the bare
lower parts and, at the same time, uses
the honeysuckle as a support.

Balsam Pear
Momordica charantia Cucurbitaceae

The genus *Momordica comprises* some 60 species, most of them distributed in tropical and subtropical Africa and Asia. They are twining herbaceous plants with long tendrils. They produce predominantly yellow flowers, which appear according to the time of sowing, usually from June to August.

Momordica balsamina is found in the wild in Africa, its range extending to north-western India, but it was also introduced to Australia and tropical America. It is an annual, about 1.5 m (5 ft) high, with deeply lobed leaves. The broadly ovate fruits with a wrinkled and wart-covered surface are green, turning orange-yellow on ripening.

Momordica charantia is an annual up to 2 m (6 ft) high, native to the Old World tropics, where it is grown as a vegetable. It can be grown outside in the subtropical regions of southern Europe, or under glass. It is sown very early in spring in a heated propagating frame and the young plants are transferred to their permanent site in late spring. A construction for climbing must be provided: a wooden or bamboo stick, plastic-covered wire or strong nylon fibre.

Momordica charantia (1) is a gourd with a long growing season, and therefore can be grown successfully only in a heated greenhouse or conservatory. The fruits are up to 20 cm (8 in) long, green-white turning to orange-yellow on ripening. When the fruits ripen and the thick skin bursts open, it reveals flat beige seeds coated in scarlet-red arils (2). The fruits are harvested green and can be served as salad with meat or fish. They have a slightly bitter taste and soft texture. They can be canned like cucumbers. The fruits have been used in folk medicine for years in their lands of origin, as they contain bitter substances which have a laxative effect.

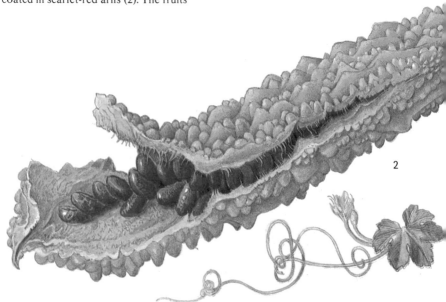

2

1

Swiss Cheese Plant, Mexican Breadfruit
Monstera deliciosa
Araceae

Some 50 species of the genus *Monstera* grow wild in tropical Central and South America. They are twining climbers with long, trailing aerial roots. In their natural habitat they climb up trees to a height of 20 m (65 ft). Only well-grown specimens produce flowers.

Monstera deliciosa is the most frequently cultivated indoor species. It is best grown alone as a specimen plant in a room or hallway, because it soon reaches a height of several metres if the conditions are favourable. Juvenile plants have entire leaves without holes, but approximately from the fourth leaf the blades are perforated and/or deeply incised. Older plants have to be tied to a support. These plants can be cultivated hydroponically.

Monstera is a relatively undemanding and vigorous-growing plant, withstanding the dry air of centrally-heated homes and offices. It can be kept at a temperature between 8 to 30 °C (46 to 86 °F), but it succeeds best at about 20 °C (68 °F). In a light position the leaves are larger and have shorter internodes.

Young plants should be repotted annually, the older ones at least once in three years, in a soil-based potting compost. Feed weekly in summer and clean the leaves regularly with water. Watering is reduced in winter because less light makes the leaves grow smaller and softer.

Propagation is by air layering, stem or tip cuttings with three leaves or so. Leaf bud cuttings, 5 to 8 cm (2 to 3 in) long can also be taken and put in a propagating frame to take root. Aerial roots should not be removed.

Monstera deliciosa (1) is native to Mexico. The leaf blades of adult plants are up to 80 cm (32 in) long. The cultivar 'Borsighiana' has a more slender trunk and smaller, less perforated leaves and longer internodes. More delicate and slow-growing cultivars with white-streaked foliage are also available.

The inflorescence, a spadix, is about 20 cm (8 in) long (2). The fruit, when it forms, is cylindrical and tasty to eat. It used to serve as food for the indigenous population in regions of Mexico where it grew wild. The fruits disintegrate on ripening, liberating the individual berries which contain seeds.

Monstera obliqua (3) originates in Brazil. It is more delicate and must be cultivated in a tropical window or heated conservatory with a temperature of 18 to 20 °C (64 to 68 °F) and high atmospheric humidity. The leaf blades measure only 20 to 30 cm (8 to 12 in).

3

2

1

137

Pitcher Plants
Nepenthes hybrids

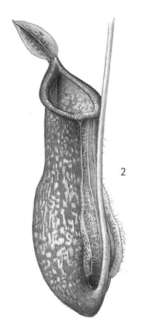

Nepenthaceae

The genus *Nepenthes* contains some 75 species and a great number of hybrids. Their natural area of distribution is the warm, humid forests of Indonesia, the Malay Peninsula, Oceania and Madagascar. They are sub-shrubs with long stems clinging to a support by means of leaf tendrils.

Most species are of interest only to collectors; they cannot be easily cultivated. The plants most commonly seen are hybrids.

Pitcher plants thrive in a warm greenhouse or terrarium with a temperature of at least 20 °C (68 °F), even in winter. They need a high atmospheric humidity and a light position shaded from direct sun. If provided with good drainage, they can be grown in clay pots. They benefit from frequent mist-spraying and occasional feeding from spring to summer. They do not tolerate lime in water or soil.

They should be transplanted each spring in a well-drained, acid compost of fibrous peat, peat moss or perlite. The delicate roots must not be damaged during repotting. As soon as the plants take root, the new shoots above the sixth to eighth leaf are pinched out, because the most beautiful pitchers are formed on the lower parts. These nipped-out shoots can be used as cuttings. These will root in foam-rubber cubes enveloped in peat moss kept in a heated propagating frame at an optimum temperature of between 25 to 30 °C (77 to 86 °F), with atmospheric humidity of 100 per cent.

2

Nepenthes hybrids (1) have the tip of the leaf elongated into a tendril, terminated by a pitcher closed with a lid that clings to the pitcher, only opening when the pitcher matures. The thickened rim of the pitcher is equipped with glands which exude nectar. Insects lured by the sweet nectar slip into the pitcher and glide down on the smooth inner sides, ending up in the enzyme-rich liquid with which

one third of the pitcher is filled. The
insects try to escape, crawl on the inner
wall and irritate the glands, which then
produce more liquid and the drowned
insects and other tiny animals are broken
down into nutrients the plants can digest.

Most of the cultivars grown have not
been named. They bear beautifully shaped
and coloured pitchers, sometimes up to
40 cm (16 in) long (2).

1

Virginia Creeper
Parthenocissus quinquefolia

Vitaceae

Parthenocissus quinquefolia, in older botanical literature listed as *Ampelopsis hederacea,* is a wild plant of the margins of light woods in the eastern United States. It reaches a height of 10 m (33 ft) under European conditions. It was introduced to Britain in 1829.

Virginia Creeper is a vigorous woody species which will quickly cover a tall wall or fence. It is grown in well-aerated, fairly deep and not too dry garden soil to which some well rotted compost has been added. It tolerates shade and dusty environments.

Bare-rooted plants should be planted in spring, while those with a soil ball can be set out in any season, unless, of course, the soil is frozen. The parts above the ground are cut back to encourage branching. At least two applications of a fertilizer during the growing period are beneficial to promote luxuriant growth. Young shoots are tied to sticks or other supports until they are able to attach themselves. In the following years pruning is restricted to the removal of shoots covering windows or getting in the way. This species tolerates heavy pruning rather well.

Parthenocissus quinquefolia is propagated by hardwood cuttings struck at the beginning of winter and stored in a frost-proof place. In spring they are transferred to a nursery bed to form roots.

Parthenocissus quinquefolia (1) holds onto its support with twining tendrils. Young shoots are reddish at first, changing to deep grey with age. The leaflets are up to 10 cm (4 in) long, yellow in autumn and later turning bright red and finally purple. The flowers are tiny and inconspicuous, borne in terminal panicles (2, 3) in July and August. They are succeeded by green, spherical berries (2). When these ripen they are bluish-black, downy, up to 5 mm (¼ in) long and have an acrid taste. Each berry contains two to three seeds.

Parthenocissus quinquefolia 'Engelmannii' (4) has longer and narrower leaf blades than the original species, with bluish undersides. They turn a red-brown colour in autumn. The tendrils are terminated by adhesive disks and can hold fast even to a marble wall.

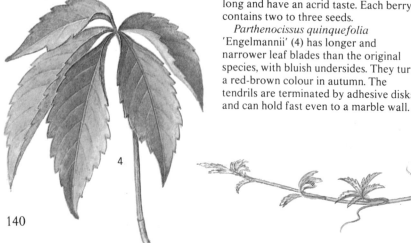

4

2

1

3

141

Boston Ivy
Parthenocissus tricuspidata   Vitaceae

Parthenocissus tricuspidata comes from Japan, Korea and central China. It is a popular garden plant used to cover a house front or a high wall. This species clings to the support by means of short and much-branched tendrils terminated by large adhesive disks which cling even to very smooth surfaces.

Parthenocissus tricuspidata 'Gloire de Boskoop' is a vigorously growing cultivar, grown for over half a century, producing large leaves turning reddish-brown in autumn. *P. tricuspidata* 'Veitchii', also known as *Ampelopsis veitchii* or *Vitis inconstans* 'Purpurea', has smaller leaves than the species and bronze-red shoots. It attains a height of 8 m (26 ft). Any damage they may suffer in harsh winters will not be serious as new shoots develop quickly from below. Both the species and its cultivars are grafted on rooted cuttings of the Virginia Creeper in February or March. The scions are taken from thicker one-year-old shoots. The lower buds on the stocks have to be removed to prevent these from sprouting instead of the scions. The pots are then placed in a greenhouse or frame. They are later planted out in their permanent sites. Layering can also be tried in the garden, but plants on their own roots grow less vigorously than those that have been grafted.

3

Parthenocissus tricuspidata (1) is a self-clinging, densely branched creeper growing to 10 m (33 ft) in height. In June and July it bears small insignificant flowers emitting a faint perfume. The flowers are followed by pea-sized green berries which turn bluish-black on ripening (2).

The deciduous, three-lobed leaves are up to 20 cm (8 in) long. In autumn, they gradually change colour from pale yellow to purple, the shade becoming noticeably different every day (3). After the leaves have been shed, the wall or fence still looks attractive, as the many-branched stems covering the surface of the wall are highly decorative. The only problem arises when the wall has to be repaired; then each branch must be torn off.

2

1

Blue Passion Flower
Passiflora caerulea   Passifloraceae

The genus *Passiflora* contains over 400 species of predominantly climbing shrubs occurring in tropical and subtropical America. Some of them are grown as crops in Asia, Africa, Australia and Polynesia. They are climbers with numerous tendrils growing from the stems. These cling to trees or other supports. The flowers usually have showy and bizarre shapes.

Passiflora caerulea can be grown in a cool greenhouse or conservatory. At first it should be tied to a support, but it will soon cling on with its spiral tendrils. In protected areas in the south, these plants survive winter out-of-doors. They should be planted against a warm, sunny wall.

Indoors passion flowers require plenty of light and fresh air. They flower poorly in semi-shade. In summer they can be placed outside on a balcony or terrace, or plunged in the ground in their pots.

At the time of full growth and flowering, regular watering is important, as well as occasional feeding with compound fertilizer. The plants are left to rest during November and December. They should spend the winter in a light place at a temperature of 8 to 10 °C (46 to 50 °F) with moderate watering. All stronger shoots should be cut back heavily before the new growths appear, to encourage the formation of new flowering shoots; passion flowers bloom on new wood.

Passiflora caerulea (1), a native of the tropical regions of southern Brazil, Argentina and Paraguay, is often grown as a house plant or outside in mild areas. The leaf blades are up to 15 cm (6 in) long. The broad buds (2) open successively from May to September to produce beautifully scented flowers of interesting shape, 6 to 10 cm (2 ¼ to 4 in) across. Five thick sepals are arranged in a star and coloured the same as the corolla, which is composed of five petals and fused with the sepals to form a bowl shape. From this grows the corona formed by a ring of long filaments.

A long central column carries five
stamens and a pistil terminated by three
styles and mallet-like stigmas. The
cultivar 'Constance Elliot' has larger
flowers and sepals with a deeper pink
tinge than the species.

1

Granadilla
Passiflora edulis

Passiflora edulis is a tender passion flower from Brazil. It is cultivated for its tasty fruit, up to 8 cm (4 in) across, in many tropical and
subtropical regions of South America, Africa, Australia, Polynesia
and south-eastern Asia.

In Britain it can be grown outside only in the mildest of gardens. It
is therefore most usually grown in greenhouses and conservatories,
because it requires plenty of warmth, light and atmospheric moisture.
The same conditions have to be provided during the winter months,
otherwise leaf drop occurs. They bloom less profusely than *Passiflora
caerulea* but the flowers have an equally exotic appearance.

It is easily propagated from seed. Without removing the arils, the
seeds can be sown in boxes, where they germinate within two or three
weeks at a temperature of 16 to 20 °C (60 to 68 °F). The seedlings are
pricked out into larger pots. Cuttings put out roots in a mixture of
sand and peat in a propagating frame kept at a temperature between
24 to 26 °C (75 to 78 °F) in three to four weeks. The Granadilla uses
wires for support like the Grape Vine.

Passiflora incarnata comes from North America. It is a perennial
growing to a height of 10 m (33 ft) under favourable conditions. The
flowers are about 4 cm (1½ in) across, white, flushed red. They appear from May to July. The plants are cultivated in a cool greenhouse
or conservatory.

2

146

Passiflora edulis (1) has leaves up to 13 cm (5 in) long. The flowers (2) are 7 cm (2 ¾ in) across, white with a purple pattern. They appear mainly from June to August. The fruits have a skin about 5 mm (¼ in) thick, pulpy at first but later becoming hard; they are spherical, some 7 cm (2 ¾ in) across, yellow or purple-violet. They ripen two or three months after the end of flowering and contain a number of deep violet seeds coated in yellow arils. The highly aromatic, pleasantly sour juice is either sucked directly from the fruits or obtained by machine-pressing them. The juice is dehydrated and resulting powder is used for the manufacture of aromatic refreshing beverages. This substance was in the past commonly used in Europe to dye and flavour confectionery products.

Giant Granadilla
Passiflora quadrangularis

Passifloraceae

Passiflora quadrangularis is a native of tropical South America. This species also yields yellow-green to reddish fruits weighing up to 2 kg (4 ½ lb). Although they are less tasty than the fruits of *P. edulis,* they are consumed in the tropics and used for the manufacturing of juice. The tubers also serve as food for the local population.

Passiflora quadrangularis is grown in a warm greenhouse or conservatory at a temperature of at least 20 °C (68 °F). A six-week period in a temperature of 15 °C (59 °F) is necessary in January and February, so that the plant can form new flower buds. It is tolerant of heavy pruning. Early spring is the best time for repotting in a soil-based potting compost when the plants are cut back to four to eight buds. Passion flowers need a support for climbing. Sticks are used in pots with young plants, and older specimens are tied to training wires or other constructions. Staking should be done early, while the plants are still flexible.

All passion flowers can be propagated by softwood cuttings. These are inserted by three in small pots placed in a propagating frame, where they will root within three weeks if kept at a temperature of 20 to 22 °C (68 to 71 °F). Stem cuttings with two buds taken from shoots of ripened wood also root readily.

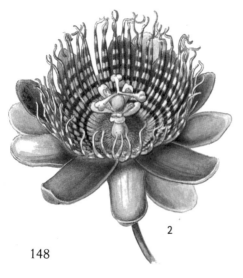

Passiflora quadrangularis (1) has a markedly quadrangular, winged stem, in its native habitat it attains a height of around 30 m (100 ft). The leaves are broadly ovate with long stalks; from the leaf axils grow long, spiral tendrils. Because of its massive growth, this species can be used only where there is plenty of space.

The flowers are also large, usually up to 13 cm (5 in) across, and vividly coloured (2). They give off a strong, spicy fragrance. Unfortunately they are short-lived when cut. Even well-developed buds will not open after cutting, so this fascinating plant cannot be used in flower arrangements.

2

1

Passiflora suberosa

The genus of passion flowers also offers some less known annuals or perennials.

Passiflora alata, a perennial species of vigorous habit, originates in Brazil and Peru. It has carmine-red, fragrant blossoms, 8 to 10 cm (3 to 4 in) across, with a white corona streaked red. These open from April to August and are followed by large berries, tasty and much-prized tropical fruits. This species can be grown in a greenhouse or conservatory in Britain.

Passiflora bryonioides is an annual with three-lobed, pure green leaves, some 8 cm (3 in) across. In July and September it produces a number of 2.5 cm (1 in) wide, white flowers with a purple stripe on the corona. The flowers are replaced by spherical berries, 2 cm ($^3/_4$ in) wide, containing seeds. These seeds are sown in February in a mixture of sand and peat. The seedlings are pricked out as soon as possible and planted into pots by twos or threes.

Passiflora racemosa is a warmth-loving species from Brazil. It has three-lobed leaves up to 13 cm (5 in) wide. The purple-red flowers with down-curved petals and a white-blue corona appear successively in racemes from May to September. The blossoms have 8 to 13 cm (3 to 5 in) in diameter.

Passiflora trifasciata is a Peruvian perennial, suitable for a warm, light position. The leaves are longish-ovate, three-lobed, with a reddish-brown flush and silvery-grey pattern along the main veins and purple on the undersides. The fragrant, tiny, yellowish flowers appear in July and August.

Passiflora suberosa (1) is also native to tropical South America. It is a lush-growing perennial suited for warm greenhouses. The leaves are predominantly three-lobed. It produces masses of greenish flowers, about 1 cm ($^1/_2$ in) across (2). They appear from June to August and are followed by green berries which change to bluish-black and reach a size of 1 cm ($^1/_2$ in) (3).

All the plants listed above require a light and airy site. The perennial species need a temperature of about 15 °C (59 °F) and reduced watering in the winter months. Since they produce a great number of leaves, they benefit from an occasional feed with a weak

1

3

solution of a compound fertilizer during the growing season. Heavy pruning is necessary in spring before the onset of new growth, to promote the formation of new shoots and a profusion of flower buds.

Ivy-leaved Geranium
Pelargonium peltatum

Geraniaceae

The genus *Pelargonium* comprises some 240 species, all native to southern Africa. They are densely branched sub-shrubs with five-petalled flowers appearing mainly from June to October.

Pelargonium peltatum was brought to Europe in 1701. Since then, it has been crossed with other species of pelargonium and yielded a number of handsome cultivars. They are light-loving plants tolerant of full sun. They thrive in a soil-based compost. Pelargoniums are planted outside in the second half of May. They must be watered regularly during growth, and well-rooted plants can be fed monthly with a compound fertilizer. The fading inflorescences and any yellowish leaves must be removed.

In winter the plants require plenty of light, fresh air and an optimum temperature of 6 to 8 °C (43 to 46 °F). Watering is reduced to prevent premature sprouting, but care must be taken not to let the roots dry out. At the end of winter they are transplanted into standard soil-based compost, any weak and diseased shoots are removed, and watering is gradually increased. Propagation is by softwood cuttings, taken either in spring or summer. The cuttings are left to wilt for a few hours and then planted in small pots filled with a sandy compost. They should root within three weeks in a well-lit place with a temperature of about 20 °C (68 °F) and slightly higher atmospheric humidity.

1

Pelargonium peltatum hybrids are multiple crosses of *P. peltatum, P. lateripes* and other species from the coastal areas of south-east Africa. The plants that are several years old have much-branched stems of drooping habit, about 75 cm (30 in) long. They are good subjects for window and balcony boxes and hanging baskets, flourishing mainly in protected balconies or loggias, where they will not suffer from rain damage.

The most common cultivars have pink flowers, others produce red or violet blossoms. The most popular cultivars include 'Berliner Balkon', reddish-pink; 'Amethyst', violet, semi-double (1); 'Lachskönigin', salmon-red, semi-double; 'Morgenlicht', pinkish-red (2); 'Rouletta', white edged and striped with red, single; 'Mauve Beauty', deep mauve, double, and 'Ville de Paris', which is a pale pink and single (3).

2

3

Peperomia scandens

The large genus *Peperomia* contains over 600 species. They occur mainly in tropical rain-forests of South America. They are evergreen, creeping or climbing perennials or semi-shrubs, often epiphytic in the wild.

Peperomia scandens, often referred to as *P. serpens,* is a native of Peru. It is a good subject for warm rooms and does well even in homes with dry air. Excessive humidity is detrimental to its growth. These qualities make it suitable for planting in mixed arrangements. It is very effective growing over a piece of branchwood, and in a large arrangement it can be used as a ground plant, or as a trailing plant in a wall container or hanging basket.

The trailing species succeed best at a temperature of about 20 °C (68 °F), in a partly shaded position. Even in winter the temperature should not drop below 18 °C (64 °F). Regular watering is important in summer. Cultivars with variegated foliage need more light, while the green-leaved species does well in semi-shade. The plants given too much nitrogen fertilizer start growing only green leaves.

Propagation is easy, from softwood cuttings with three to four leaves taken in early spring or late summer. The cuttings take two to three weeks to root if provided with bottom heat set at 22 to 25 °C (71 to 77 °F), shade and a moderately moist compost.

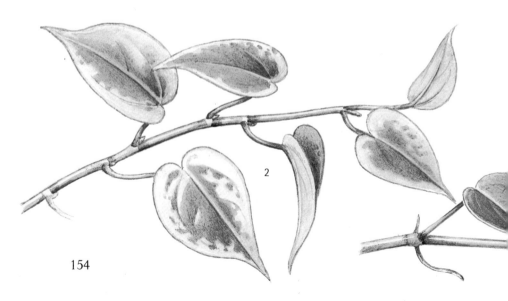

2

Peperomia scandens (1) has succulent leaves 4 to 5 cm (1 ½ to 2 in) long. The leaf blade is asymmetrical, slightly curved like a scythe blade. The species has olive-green foliage. The elongated, spiky inflorescence with creamy-white blossoms appears in summer. The cultivars with white-streaked leaves are very popular, like *P. s.* 'Variegata' (2). *P. scandens* and its variegated cultivars frequently suffer from leaf drop, caused mainly by the drying out of the root ball. The damaged shoots then have to be cut back above the second or third bud, the plant has to be given some fresh compost, moved to a lighter spot, and watered and fed regularly.

1

155

Petunia
Petunia × *hybrida*

Solanaceae

Petunias are annual and perennial plants growing wild in South America in about 25 species. *Petunia* × *hybrida* is the common name for all cultivars resulting from cross-breeding of *P. axillaris* (syn. *P. nyctaginiflora*) and *P. violacea*. Over a century and a half, many cultivars have been bred, differing in habit, colour, shape of flowers and other features. These cultivars are grouped according to form and habit. The group Pendula comprises the trailing, profusely flowering cultivars with shoots up to 60 cm (24 in) long. The flowers are about 7 cm (2 ¾ in) across, with unfringed margins. They are resistant to rain and heat, but like other petunias they are tender.

They can be planted out in the second half of May when their flowers begin to open. They require plenty of sunshine and ample watering. An occasional dose of diluted compound fertilizer is advisable. The withering flowers must be removed regularly to avoid seeds forming and encourage flowering.

The seeds are sown under glass in February, in seed compost. The seeds are very fine. Germination takes place within 10 to 14 days. After the growth of the second leaf the seedlings are pricked out into pots which are placed in a hothouse or greenhouse until they are planted out.

4   3

2

The trailing cultivars can be used in
hanging baskets and window boxes or
other containers from mid-May to the
first autumn frosts. The boxes have to be
wide and deep enough to provide space
for roots to grow. The plants branch
naturally and although they are erect at
first, the long stems with funnel-shaped
flowers soon begin to droop. Petunias
come in countless cultivars with flowers
coloured red, mauve, pink, salmon and
white. Some of the latest cultivars have
yellow flowers. The most popular
petunias include 'Magentarot',
carmine-red (1); 'Lavina', pure white (2);
'Feuerschein', fiery red (3); 'Violacea',
blue-violet (4) and the Cascades.

Scarlet Runner Bean
Phaseolus coccineus   Leguminosae

The genus *Phaseolus* contains some 200 species native to tropical America and southern Asia. Some are grown as vegetables.

Phaseolus coccineus cultivars are best known as the vegetable Runner Bean but the species can also be used as an ornamental annual to cover fences, dividing walls and espaliers. It is commonly planted against the supporting columns of pergolas or other garden constructions. It is one of the most rewarding annuals to train over balcony and loggia walls.

Beans prefer deep, well-drained, rich soil and a sunny and warm position. They need support in the form of sticks, wires, strings or wire netting. They are fast growers and soon form a dense green wall. They tend, however, to become unattractive after flowering. This has to be borne in mind when growing them in a balcony box; they should be sown in succession, the withered plants removed and replaced by younger ones.

Beans can be sown directly in planting holes in their permanent site starting from the beginning of May, three seeds to a hole. The seeds should germinate within nine days. For an early planting, they can be sown under glass in small pots, and planted out after the danger of spring frosts is over. Plenty of water in the soil is necessary at the time of maximum growth and flowering. No feeding is required.

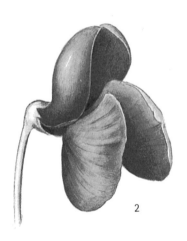

2

Phaseolus coccineus, a Mexican climber with an anticlockwise twining stem growing up to 4 m (13 ft) high, is an ornamental annual. The species has been superceded by cultivars with red, white or bi-coloured flowers. The cultivars with red-white flowers, such as *P. coccineus* 'Bicolor' (1), are of the highest ornamental value. Less frequent are cultivars with single-coloured flowers, like 'Scharlachrote Riesen' with scarlet-red flowers (2) or the creamy-white 'Albiflora'. The young legumes (3) are much better known as vegetables. The seeds of ornamental beans show a variety of colours, which are typical features of individual cultivars. *P. coccineus* 'Bicolor' has multicoloured seeds (4).

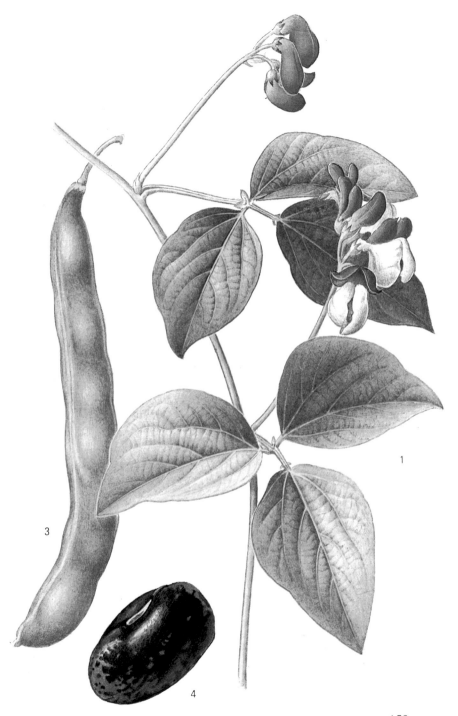

1

3

4

159

Heart-leaf Philodendron, Sweetheart Plant
Philodendron scandens
Araceae

The genus *Philodendron* comprises some 250 species of climbers found in the rain-forests of tropical America. Some species are shrubby, most, however, are climbers. The stem produces aerial roots which cling to a support and absorb humidity from the air. When damaged, the tissues exude white latex. The flowerhead takes the form of an elongated spike with both female and male flowers. It is protected by a white, yellow or red sheath, in some species reaching a length of 30 cm (12 in).

Philodendron scandens is one of the most popular house plants, undemanding and rewarding even for a beginner. The plants are tied to a stick or some trellis or grown over a piece of branchwood. For short-term purposes they can be used in planting combinations, although it is difficult to select companions as undemanding in terms of environment and treatment.

Philodendron erubescens is native to Colombia. It is a climbing, vigorous species with leaves up to 35 cm (14 in) long. It is tolerant of excesses in temperature. The cultivar 'Burgundy' is of a more compact growth and the leaves are a deeper red.

Philodendron melanochrysum in another Colombian species. Young plants have leaf blades about 10 cm (4 in) long, older specimens have leaves up to 80 cm (32 in) in length. This is the most demanding climbing philodendron, suitable mainly for a heated conservatory or sun room.

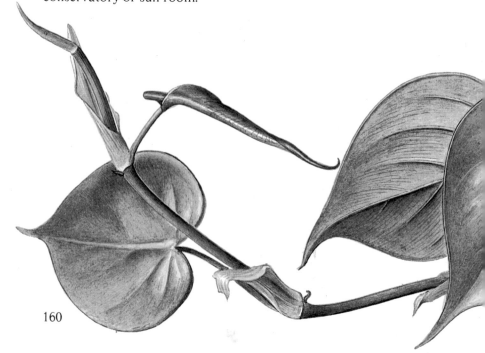

Philodendron scandens (1), often still listed as *P. oxycardium*, is widely distributed throughout Central and South America. It is the most common house philodendron. It is grown only in its juvenile form with leaves 8 to 15 cm (3 to 6 in) long (2). It needs a winter temperature of 10 to 22 °C (50 to 71 °F) and some atmospheric humidity; it benefits from regular misting. In summer it has to be sheltered from direct sunlight. The cultivar 'Variegatum' has white-splashed leaves.

The stems of climbing philodendrons are often allowed to twine around moss sticks which should be kept damp at all times. The aerial roots penetrate the peat moss and draw out moisture. Philodendrons can also be grown hydroponically.

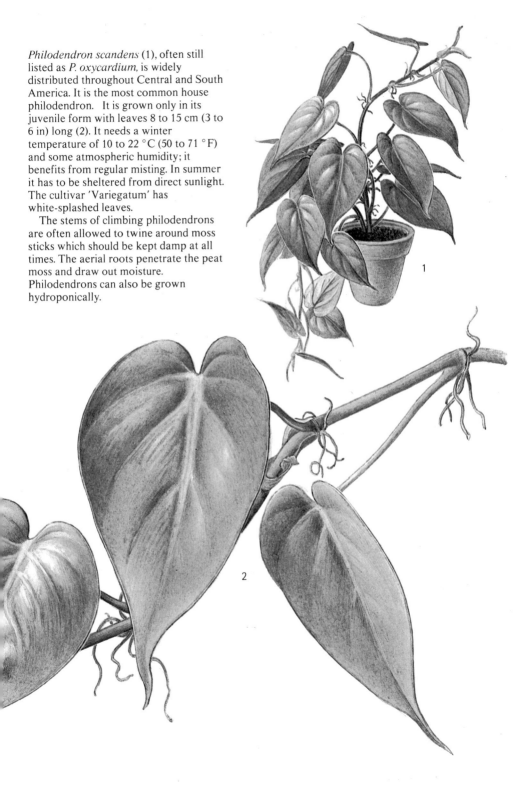

Philodendron squamiferum belongs to the group of climbing species with lobed leaves. It grows wild in the humus-rich soils of tropical rain-forests in eastern South America. The leaf blade measures up to 50 cm (20 in) in length and 35 cm (14 in) in width. This species is comparatively demanding as to temperature and humidity. It succeeds best in a heated greenhouse or conservatory. It prefers diffused light to direct sun. Unless copiously watered at the time of full growth, it tends to produce smaller leaves. A compound fertilizer should be applied monthly from April to August. Watering in winter is reduced to prevent the formation of new leaves which would be smaller and more tender than in summer, but the root ball must not be allowed to dry out.

All philodendrons are repotted as necessary, preferably in early spring, into a peat-based potting compost.

Philodendrons are usually increased by softwood cuttings, if possible with three well-developed leaves and at least one aerial root. They are pricked singly into pots filled with peat and sand. They form roots within four to eight weeks if placed in a propagating frame kept at a temperature of 22 to 25 °C (71 to 77 °F) with high humidity. However, *P. scandens* will root readily in a glass of water.

Philodendron squamiferum (1) is a vigorous species with creeping stems that turn woody. The leaf stalks in the juvenile state are covered with red scales, up to 1 cm (1/2 in) long, changing to green with age. Even relatively young plants bear purple-red flowers in spring or summer.

2

Philodendron laciniatum (2), sometimes still described as *P. amazonicum,* has a range of distribution along the borders of Brazil and Venezuela. Its stem grows slowly and bears short aerial roots. The winter temperature in cultivation should not drop below 15 °C (59 °F). Like other philodendrons, it requires high atmospheric humidity, and it can be best situated in a large conservatory or heated greenhouse. It benefits from regular misting, especially in summer. It does not undergo a marked period of rest from growth.

1

Artillery Plant
Pilea microphylla Urticaceae

There are around 200 species of the genus *Pilea* growing in the wild chiefly in tropical regions of southern Asia and South America. They are mostly perennials, often of creeping habit.

Pilea microphylla, still occasionally referred to as *P. muscosa*, is distributed in the wild in the South American Andes, but it has also been introduced to and naturalized in the Balkans. It is grown as a house plant thriving even in partially shaded positions. In the summer months it can be stood outside in the garden in a semi-shaded position. It is used in mixed plantings and as ground-cover for terrariums or in larger arrangements.

Pilea nummulariifolia is a South American species which deserves greater popularity. The creeping shoots of this undemanding plant put out roots readily when touching the ground. In mixed plants their shoots will spill over the edges of the containers. They can also be used in hanging baskets.

Both species are dependable plants tolerating a wide temperature range, from 6 to 25 °C (43 to 77 °F). They prefer semi-shade because their leaves turn yellow in direct sun. Watering is reduced according to temperature during the winter. Softwood cuttings soon send out roots if placed in water. Young plants are grown in a soil-based compost in small pots or shallow bowls. They are pinched back from an early age to promote branching.

Pilea microphylla (1) is a perennial of creeping habit, soon forming a dense, pale green carpet. The many-branched stems bear a number of sessile, fleshy leaflets, only about 5 mm (1/4 in) long, reminiscent of some ferns. Since the Artillery Plant is low growing, it is used as a ground cover or edging plant in mixed arrangements. The tiny white blossoms (2) are inconspicuous and open from May to September.

Pilea nummulariifolia (3) is also an
evergreen, creeping plant, forming
a number of long, thin stems with
roundish leaves, 2 to 3 cm (about 1 in)
long, and covered with fine hairs on both
sides. The leaves resemble those of the
Ground Ivy, *Glechoma hederacea.*

Pepper
Piper nigrum   Piperaceae

Over 700 species of pepper plants are distributed in the Asian and American tropics, and on the Pacific islands. All are warmth-loving woody species requiring high atmospheric humidity. The variegated forms are the most sensitive to temperature.

Pepper is grown for its fruit in tropical plantations in warm humid climates. It has been occasionally grown as a house plant for a long time. It can be used as a climber trained over trellis or pieces of branchwood, or as a trailing plant in wall containers, or as a ground-cover in a large mixed planting.

Pepper is an undemanding plant succeeding indoors or under glass at high temperatures and humid conditions. It needs a winter temperature of 16 to 18 °C (61 to 64 °F) and regular watering. However, it will not tolerate waterlogged compost, and so excessive water has to be tipped away from the saucer. On warm days the plants benefit from occasional misting over with water. A fortnightly application of a compound fertilizer is recommended in spring and summer. These plants should be potted in a soil-based compost. They are repotted in spring. Since the lower stems often become bare, some of them should be shortened annually to produce new shoots.

Piper nigrum (1) probably originates from south-western India, but it is widely cultivated for its fruit throughout tropical Asia. The stems with a woody base are up to 7 m (23 ft) long and produce numerous aerial roots from their nodes. The aerial roots send out more roots where they touch the ground. The evergreen, slightly leathery leaves are about 8 cm (3 in) long and lighter in colour on their undersides.

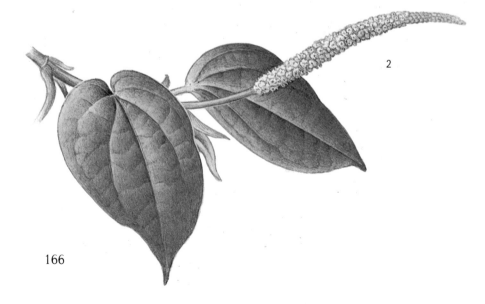

2

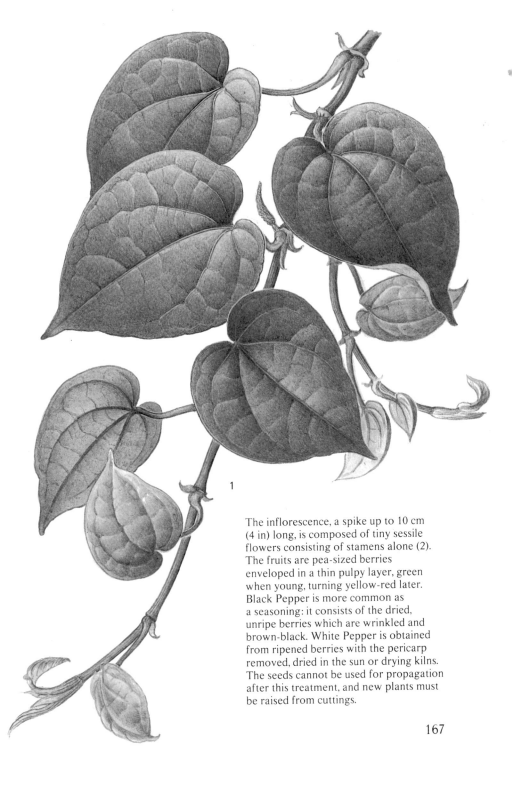

1

The inflorescence, a spike up to 10 cm
(4 in) long, is composed of tiny sessile
flowers consisting of stamens alone (2).
The fruits are pea-sized berries
enveloped in a thin pulpy layer, green
when young, turning yellow-red later.
Black Pepper is more common as
a seasoning: it consists of the dried,
unripe berries which are wrinkled and
brown-black. White Pepper is obtained
from ripened berries with the pericarp
removed, dried in the sun or drying kilns.
The seeds cannot be used for propagation
after this treatment, and new plants must
be raised from cuttings.

Piper ornatum

Piper ornatum is a relatively demanding, highly decorative perennial. It does best in a heated greenhouse or conservatory with high atmospheric humidity. *P. porphyrophyllum* is a climber from the Malay Peninsula. The evergreen leaves are spotted in the juvenile stage, later become olive-brown with pink spots, and reddish on the underside.

Both these species are native to the tropical rain-forests and therefore need a higher temperature and atmospheric humidity. They require light shade. There is no marked period of rest from growth. Because of the lower light intensity in winter, they tolerate a decrease in temperature to 18 °C (64 °F) provided watering is also reduced. A low temperature and waterlogging of the compost can kill the plant. Both species require plenty of nutrients and at the time of full growth they must be given a fortnightly application of a fertilizer.

Pepper plants are usually multiplied from softwood or stem cuttings with two buds, best taken in February and March. Three to five cuttings are put in an 8-cm (3-in) pot. For successful rooting they need to be placed in a propagating frame with a bottom heat of 22 to 25 °C (71 to 77 °F) and misted frequently. The rooted cuttings should have their tips pinched out at an early stage to obtain densely branched plants. The plants are potted on as necessary.

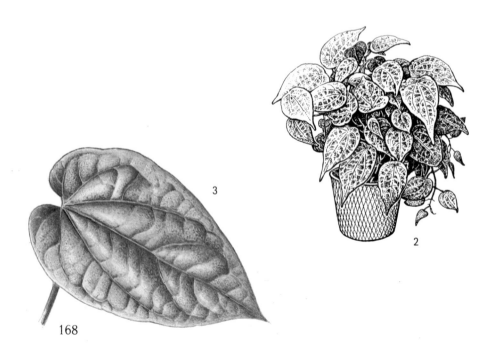

3

2

168

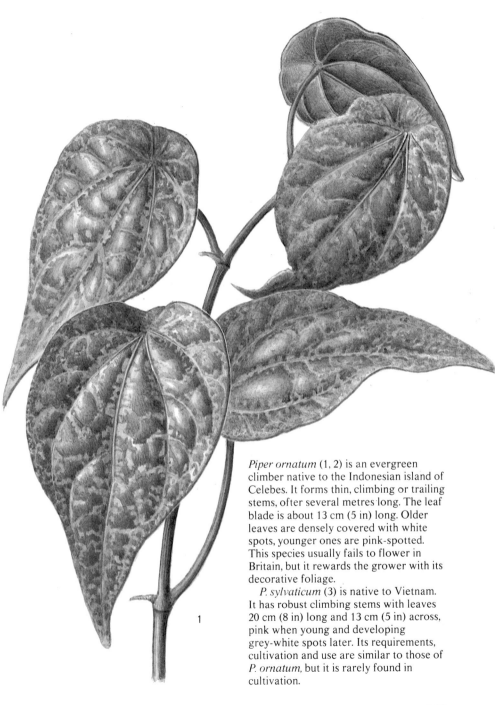

Piper ornatum (1, 2) is an evergreen
climber native to the Indonesian island of
Celebes. It forms thin, climbing or trailing
stems, often several metres long. The leaf
blade is about 13 cm (5 in) long. Older
leaves are densely covered with white
spots, younger ones are pink-spotted.
This species usually fails to flower in
Britain, but it rewards the grower with its
decorative foliage.

P. sylvaticum (3) is native to Vietnam.
It has robust climbing stems with leaves
20 cm (8 in) long and 13 cm (5 in) across,
pink when young and developing
grey-white spots later. Its requirements,
cultivation and use are similar to those of
P. ornatum, but it is rarely found in
cultivation.

Cape Leadwort
Plumbago capensis   Plumbaginaceae

Some 10 species of the small genus *Plumbago* have been discovered so far in tropical and subtropical regions of Africa and Asia.

Plumbago capensis, often listed as *P. auriculata,* is usually grown in a large container or in a greenhouse border. It should spend the winter in a cool, frostproof and light place, at an optimum temperature of 4 to 8 °C (39 to 46 °F). From the end of May it can be situated on a balcony, terrace or other suitable outdoor place. They like a sheltered site with plenty of sunshine, but the root ball should be shaded. The plants have to be taken inside in autumn.

Plumbago as a climber is generally grown in an unheated greenhouse, tied to trellis or strung wires. It can be trained from a single shoot into a tree-like form with a sparse crown within a few years; the plant must be tied to a support and have the lower branches removed.

In the growing season the plants require plenty of water and an occasional feed. Watering is reduced in winter but the soil must never become dried out. At the end of February the shoots are shortened to half their length and the plants are transferred to a warm place and allowed to sprout. They can also be repotted in a peat-based potting compost at the same time.

Softwood cuttings are used for propagation in May, cuttings of ripe wood in August or September. They root in a propagating frame at a temperature of between 16 and 18 °C (60 and 64 °F). The plants grown from seed flower a year later than those raised from cuttings.

Plumbago capensis (1) is a climbing shrub from southern Africa. The leaves are deciduous and up to 5 cm (2 in) long. The long, climbing or trailing branches are covered with a multitude of flowers grouped in semi-spherical inflorescences throughout the summer. The individual flowers (2) have a narrow tube enlarged into a saucer-like shape at the edge. The species has pale blue flowers, the cultivar *P. auriculata* 'Alba' bears pure white blossoms. In the mildest parts of the country the plants can remain outside in winter, provided they are given a good cover. In southern Europe, particularly along the Mediterranean Sea, *P. capensis* is used for hedging or festooning high walls and gates.

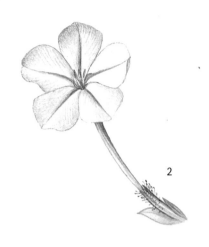

2

1

Devil's Ivy, Golden Pothos
Scindapsus aureus
Araceae

The genus *Scindapsus* includes some 20 species found chiefly in the tropical rain forest of Asia, the East Indies, New Guinea and Fiji. Their stems often climb up to treetops and they use their aerial roots for extra support.

This plant has often been reclassified from one genus to another in the last few decades. It is therefore known under many names, the most common being *Rhaphidophora aurea* and *Pothos aureus.* The most recent valid name is *Epipremnum aureum.* It is a commonly cultivated house plant. The leaves are intolerant of bright sunshine but also do poorly in a too-shady place. Unless the variegated forms are given sufficient light, the leaves turn green.

At the time of full growth the plant needs regular watering and feeding. It is repotted as necessary in a peat-based potting compost. *Scindapsus* flourishes in a warm and humid position where the temperature never drops below 18 °C (60 °F) in winter.

Propagation is usually by softwood cuttings with three or four leaves, at any season. The cuttings are put directly in a shallow pan or pot filled with peat and sand, several pieces to a pot. They root best in a propagating frame kept at a temperature of about 25 °C (80 °F).

Scindapsus aureus (1) is native to the Solomon Islands. Under favourable conditions it forms occasionally branched shoots, up to 6 m (20 ft) long, with thick aerial roots. The leaves are heart-shaped, rather asymmetrical, splashed with golden yellow (2 — underside of the leaf). They are thin, about 10 cm (4 in) long and 7 cm (2 ¾ in) wide in the

juvenile state. In adult specimens the
leaf blade may be as much as 60 cm
(24 in) long and 40 cm (16 in) wide.
S. aureus 'Marble Queen' is a cultivar
variegated with white, more delicate
and less rampant than the original
species. Smaller plants are grown on
epiphytic trunks (3), placed in
terrariums or trained up
moss-covered sticks. They can be
grown hydroponically.

Climbing Rose
Rosa sp.
Rosaceae

Climbing roses with long arching branches and a multitude of beautifully coloured flowers are favourite woody species of parks and gardens. They are generally used to cover fences, house walls, pergolas and trelliswork. A garden gate looks very attractive surrounded with hundreds of rose blossoms. A support must be fastened to house walls for roses to climb on. Depending on the vigour of the cultivar, the plants are spaced 1 to 3 m (3 to 10 ft) apart. Climbing roses can also be grown without support, planted on slopes as ground cover.

Like other species and cultivars of the same genus, climbing roses need good garden soil and a sunny site. They flourish only when given adequate moisture and rich growing conditions. The soil should have a pH of between 6.0 to 7.0. Roses produce fewer flowers when planted in the shade and their growth is weaker.

Before planting the soil should be dry to at least a spade's depth. Since a rose lasts for 15 to 20 years, the soil has to be enriched with plenty of well-rotted manure or compost. The best time for planting is during November. Roses are planted so the graft mark is no more than 2.5 cm (1 in) below ground after the soil has settled. The newly planted shrubs are given a good watering.

Climbing roses flower on old wood and so young shoots should not be cut off; only the shoots that are too old, weak or damaged are removed. The newly-planted shrubs are given fertilizer only after they have established themselves.

Climbing roses include many cultivars differing in their habit of growth, shape, colour of flowers, capacity to bloom repeatedly and hardiness.

Depending on their parentage, the cultivars are classed in groups. For instance *Wichuraiana* hybrids include 'Coral Dawn' with beautifully scented, coral-pink flowers (1); the group *Kordesii* hybrids contains 'Ilse Krohn Superior' with pure white blossoms (2), 'Leverkusen' (3) with lemon-yellow flowers and the orange-flowered 'Morgengruss' (4). In nurseries the cultivars are budded on the stock of the wild *Rosa canina*, because the plants raised from cuttings develop a poor root system.

Rubus henryi

There are some 400 species of brambles distributed predominantly in the temperate zone of the Northern Hemisphere.

Rubus henryi is native to central China. It is not commonly cultivated. This shrub prefers a semi-shaded protected position and moist soil. The above-ground parts may suffer damage from frost in a harsh winter, but the shrub will usually shoot again from below in spring. In mild regions it can be planted on the top of a terrace wall, or trained over a dividing wall or up a post or arch in the garden. It also makes a good subject for covering slopes and preventing soil erosion.

Like most evergreen woody plants, brambles are bought growing in containers and are planted out, preferably in spring. The long shoots need tying to a support. This species flowers and fruits on the previous year's wood and so no pruning is necessary, with the exception of occasional thinning or cutting back.

Rubus henryi is propagated from seeds sown immediately after harvesting or after stratification in March. It can also be raised from cuttings taken in August which take root under glass. These can be planted outside the following spring. If the shrub spreads, it can also be propagated by division or root cuttings.

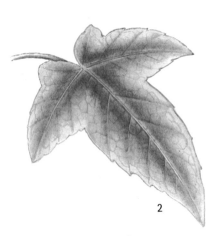

2

Rubus henryi (1) has creeping or weak climbing thorny shoots, up to 6 m (20 ft) long, with deeply-lobed evergreen leaves measuring 10 to 15 cm (4 to 6 in) in length. The racemes of pale red flowers are almost 2 cm (¾ in) across and appear in early summer. They are followed by inconspicuous black shiny fruits.

Rubus reflexus from south-eastern China is an evergreen shrub occasionally grown as a climbing greenhouse plant. The broom-like stems are densely covered with soft, rusty-brown hairs and sparse thorns. The dark green leaves have a wide, silvery-grey margin (2). *R. reflexus* requires a shady position and plenty of warmth and humidity. In winter the temperature must be at least 18 °C (64 °F) and watering has to be reduced.

1

Aaron's Beard, Mother-of-Thousands
Saxifraga stolonifera

Saxifragaceae

The genus *Saxifraga* comprises over 300 species of mostly alpine plants of the Northern Hemisphere with a small number of species in the South American Andes.

Saxifraga stolonifera, commonly known as *S. sarmentosa*, frequents slightly shaded rocky slopes in China and Japan. It has been cultivated as a pot plant in Europe since 1815. It is grown mainly in cool rooms in wall containers or hanging baskets positioned high enough to display the trailing runners which are up to 50 cm (20 in) long. The plants can also be grown hydroponically, for which purpose the baby plants are best suited. These undemanding house plants are suitable for a cool place. They do well in a winter temperature of about 10 °C (50 °F), the variegated forms doing better in a slightly higher temperature of 15 to 18 °C (59 to 64 °F). They succeed best in partial shade.

When in full growth the plants need moderate watering, but the compost must never be allowed to dry out, not even in winter. From April to July they benefit from being fed once a fortnight. Older plants are repotted once every two or three years or when necessary.

Saxifraga stolonifera is propagated from baby plants separated from the runners at any time of the year. The baby plants often send out roots when they touch the compost, while still attached to the parent plant.

The flat leaf rosettes of *Saxifraga stolonifera* send out long, flexible runners about 50 cm (20 in) long, which produce small rosettes, the baby plants. The species has green leaves with white veins, *S. stolonifera* 'Tricolor' (1) has smaller leaves variegated with pink and white and is more tender. Showy white

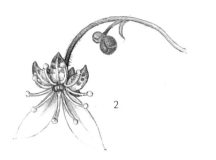

flowers appear in June and July. The inflorescence is about 30 cm (12 in) long and is composed of flowers (2) some 2 cm (¾ in) across which open in succession. Plants grown indoors rarely flower but they are worth growing for their attractive foliage.

Ivy Arum, Silver Vine
Scindapsus pictus

Araceae

Scindapsus pictus is native to Malaysia. It does best in a heated green-house, terrarium or vitrine, where it is trained over a piece of branch-wood, planted in a hanging basket, or allowed to climb a wall. It can also be used as a ground-covering subject.

This rather demanding house plant needs a temperature between 20 and 25 °C (68 to 77 °F) and a fairly humid atmosphere. The temperature must not drop below 15 °C (60 °F) in winter. A semi-shaded or shady site is best. The plants require regular watering according to season. Established plants are given a monthly feed in summer.

Scindapsus pictus can be propagated by vegetative means in any season. Stem cuttings with two to three well-developed leaves root best in spring, in a propagating frame with bottom heat of about 22 °C (71 °F). Three to five cuttings can be put in one pot in a peaty cutting compost. The ideal soil pH range is between 5.5 and 6.5.

Scindapsus pictus, in older works listed as *Pothos argyraeus,* has leathery leaves 10 to 15 cm (4 to 6 in) long. Only its juvenile form (1) is used as an ornamental plant; it does not produce flowers, and the leaves are smaller and the stems thinner than those of the adult plant. Because juvenile form has been propagated by vegetative means for so long, the fertile form has practically disappeared from cultivation.

In addition to the species, there is also the variegated cultivar *S. pictus* 'Argyraeus' (2) with smaller leaves covered with more intensely silver-white spots. The species and its cultivars can be grown hydroponically. The aerial roots should not be removed; they are used for clinging to a support and for absorbing moisture from the air.

1

2

181

Sedum sieboldii
Grassulaceae

The genus *Sedum* contains about 500 species distributed throughout Europe, Africa, North and South America. Only a few tropical and subtropical species are grown indoors.

Sedum sieboldii is a succulent plant suitable for cool rooms. The pot or container is placed in a window, preferably facing east, where the temperature stays fairly cool. It also looks attractive in a hanging basket, and it can be planted in a window box in the summer.

In the growing season sedums need careful watering, which is reduced to almost nothing in winter. This is a light-loving species, which requires a winter temperature between 5 and 8 °C (41 to 46 °F). It needs little in the way of feeding. Older plants are repotted once in two or three years if necessary, younger ones every year, in early spring. Use a soil-based potting compost with extra sharp sand added to ensure the drainage is good.

Sedums are easy to propagate by stem cuttings taken in July and August. Several cuttings can be put in one pot to form a future decorative arrangement. Single leaves can also be used for propagation. They are laid out on sandy soil and will root readily. As soon as the stems sprout, they should be transplanted into a suitably sized pot or container. They can be increased from seed, preferably in spring. The seeds germinate within two to three weeks. The seed remains viable for three years at most.

Sedum sieboldii is native to Japan. The trailing stems reach a length of 25 cm (10 in) (1) and the fleshy leaves measure about 1 cm (1/2 in) across. Umbels of tiny, pink-red, five-petalled flowers appear in autumn. In very mild areas this species can survive the winter outside if given some protection. *S. sieboldii* 'Medio-variegatum' (2) has a yellowish blotch in the middle of each leaf; the foliage contains less chlorophyll and the plant is consequently more delicate than the species.

Senecio doria (3), a succulent plant of central and southern Europe, has similar growing requirements to *Sedum sieboldii.* Its leaves are fleshy, about 1 cm (1/2 in) long. The inconspicuous composite flowers open in July and August.

3

1

2

Purple Heart
Setcreasea pallida   Commelinaceae

Only 5 species of this genus, all native to Mexico and Texas, have been discovered so far. They are perennials of mainly creeping habit.

Setcreasea pallida, commonly known under the name of *S. purpurea*, is a Mexican species. It is generally grown as a house plant in a wall container or hanging basket. During the summer it can be placed in window and balcony boxes outside, where it can also be used in the company of annuals in flower beds and borders.

The plants prefer a light, partially shaded site sheltered from direct sunshine. In a well-lit position the leaves are magnificently coloured, but direct sun and dry air cause the leaf margins to turn brown. The optimum temperature is about 22 °C (71 °F) in summer and 15 °C (59 °F) in winter. Watering must be adapted to season and temperature. It must be done with care for if water touches the leaves unsightly spots develop. Feed occasionally during summer. Young plants have much better-coloured foliage and they must be stopped frequently to promote a bushy growth.

Propagation is easy; just insert tip cuttings directly in pots filled with a peat-based compost and they root rapidly. Three to five cuttings fit in a 10-cm (4-in) pot. The cuttings will also form roots in water.

2

3

Setcreasea pallida (1) has rather thick fleshy shoots about 40 cm (16 in) long and sessile leaves up to 18 cm (7 in) long and 4 cm (1½ in) across. The plants, which are of upright habit at first, later tend to creep or droop. The inconspicuous, purple-pink flowers (2), about 1 cm (½ in) wide, appear mainly in the spring and summer, less frequently in the autumn and winter months. Plants fed a nitrogen-rich compound fertilizer grow vigorously but produce fewer flowers.

Callisia elegans (3) is also a native of Mexico. Its creeping stems with leaves up to 7 cm (2 ¾ in) long form a dense cover. It needs a winter temperature over 16 °C (60 °F). It does not tolerate drying out of the compost. Its growing requirements are similar to those of *Setcreasea pallida*.

185

Clustered Wax Flower
Stephanotis floribunda   Asclepiadaceae

The genus *Stephanotis* comprises 16 species of evergreen climbers with leathery leaves. All are found in the wild in the Malay Peninsula and Malagasy.

Stephanotis floribunda, native to Malagasy, reaches 8 m (26 ft) in height. As a house plant it requires a light position, a high atmospheric moisture and regular watering. It needs feeding once a fortnight with a low-nitrogen fertilizer. In winter it should be stored in good light with a temperature of 12 do 14 °C (53 to 57 °F) and watered sparingly.

Young plants are repotted annually, older ones every two or three years in soil- or peat-based potting compost. The optimum soil pH is 6.0 to 6.5. Any weak stems are removed in spring. The plant should be given a rest from growth to assure plenty of flowers. By controlled cultivation, i. e. by shifting the time of rest and providing exact temperature and lighting conditions, growers can induce plants to bloom at any time of the year.

Stephanotis is propagated by cuttings. Softwood cuttings are taken in early spring and inserted in a mixture of peat and sand. They take root within four or five weeks at a temperature of 25 °C (77 °F). Propagation from seed is less advantageous, because seedlings usually grow more poorly than plants raised from cuttings.

2

Stephanotis floribunda (1) has evergreen, leathery leaves about 9 cm (2 ½ in) long. The strongly-scented white flowers naturally appear from June to September. The individual blossoms are about 4 cm (1 ½ in) long and look as if made of wax (2). They are reminiscent of enlarged lilac blossoms but are arranged in a sparse umbel. Small plants are grown in a pot or bowl, trained up a stick or wire arch (3), and placed by a window. Larger and older plants with stems reaching several metres in length are situated in an unheated greenhouse, set in a spacious container or directly in the bed and trained along wires or trellis. The flowers can be used for decorative purposes either in bouquets or arrangements in vases held in position with a pin holder.

1

3

187

Five Fingers
Syngonium auritum

Araceae

There are 14 known species of *Syngonium,* all occurring in Latin America, extending from Mexico to Brazil and nearby islands. They are climbing plants forming long stems which, when damaged, exude latex which solidifies on the bark. The leaves are highly variable, often arrow-shaped in the juvenile stage, later becoming palmately lobed. The flower spike is enveloped by a differently coloured sheath. However, plants grown indoors bloom only rarely.

Syngonium auritum is one of the more common species cultivated in Europe. Smaller plants are grown in pots and trained up moss-covered sticks, or allowed to climb over a piece of branchwood. A large plant can cover a greenhouse wall or conservatory walls given the correct growing conditions.

The plants need a warm site with an optimum temperature of 20 to 22 °C (68 to 71 °F), but they tolerate brief periods at slightly lower temperatures. However, the temperature should never drop below 15 °C (59 °F), not even in winter. Direct sunshine should be avoided; the plants prefer semi-shade.

Loose, nutrient-rich soil is used for repotting. It is advisable to place the pot in a larger container or dish filled with gravel and moist peat, or to grow the plants hydroponically. It is a moisture-loving species, so regular spraying with water is beneficial.

Syngonium auritum grows wild in Mexico and Jamaica. The stems are creeping in the early stage, later become climbing and develop many aerial roots.

Young leaves are broadly lanceolate (1), developing three lobes with age. Adult plants are epiphytic. Only well-grown and properly fed plants living under favourable conditions will produce flowers (2). The spike of tiny yellow-white flowers is protected by a green, purple-flushed sheath. The fruits are red berries, usually ripening only in the native habitat of the species.

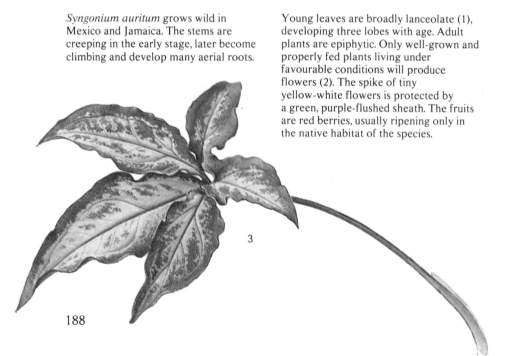

3

Syngonium podophyllum, the
Arrowhead Vine or Goosefoot Plant, also
has variable foliage. Juvenile plants form
only simple or little-divided leaves, while
many-lobed leaves appear later (3).

1

2

Arrowhead Vine, Goosefoot Plant
Syngonium podophyllum   Araceae

Syngonium podophyllum is a climber suited for warm interiors with fairly moist air. Aerial roots are a proof of healthy growth. In rooms with dry air the plants survive for only a short period. They prefer a greenhouse or conservatory. In large arrangements they can be used as ground cover.

This species is treated like the philodendrons. It requires a warm habitat and semi-shade. The optimum soil pH figure is between 5.0 to 6.5.

Syngonium podophyllum is repotted from March to August if necessary. At the time of full growth, from mid-March to the end of August, it is given a monthly feed.

Both *Syngonium podophyllum* and *S. auritum* are usually propagated by softwood or stem cuttings inserted in a mixture of leaf-mould, peat and sand in a propagator with bottom heat. The aerial roots are placed in the substrate to form roots. An amateur grower can try air layering, the method often used with rubber plants. The stem is incised and wrapped in moss which is kept moist in a polythene bag. The plants form roots in stem nodes, beneath leaf stalks. When this part of the plant has sent out roots, it can be cut off and put in a pot. Older plants sometimes form branches which can be separated and used for cultivation provided they develop their own roots.

Syngonium podophyllum grows wild from Mexico to Costa Rica. Older plants have leaves composed of three to nine leaflets, 15 to 20 cm (6 to 8 in) long (1); young leaves are arrow-shaped. The plant grows to a height of 3 m (10 ft). The great variation in shapes and colours has been made use of in breeding, and there are some recent new cultivars, such as *S. podophyllum* 'Green Gold' with green foliage and yellow-white markings. *S. podophyllum* 'Imperial White' produces silvery-white leaves changing to pale green with age. Young specimens of

the cultivar *S. podophyllum*
'Albolineatum' have an attractive
silvery-white pattern (2), but the leaves
usually turn green with age though not all
at the same time. Some plants thus carry
both variegated and green leaves.

Tetrastigma voinerianum
Vitaceae

There are 93 known species of the genus *Tetrastigma*, distributed in the wild in south-eastern Asia, Australia and on Pacific islands. They are climbers reaching a height of up to 8 m (26 ft).

Only young plants of *Tetrastigma voinerianum*, still known by the name *Vitis voinerianum*, can be grown in pots, either tied to sticks or allowed to hang down. Older specimens are robust and take up a lot of space. At first they have to be tied to a trellis or trailing wires, later they hold to the support themselves. They are able to cover a large surface in a short time, because the annual shoots are up to several metres long.

In winter the plants should be placed in a greenhouse, conservatory or spacious hallway with an optimum temperature of 15 to 18 °C (59 to 64 °F), greater atmospheric humidity and semi-shade. They are tolerant of a smoky environment.

Tetrastigma needs regular and copious watering, reduced in winter; waterlogged conditions are harmful. Fortnightly feeding with a balanced liquid fertilizer is recommended in the growing season, from April to August. This robust vigorous climber is transplanted when necessary into a soil-based potting compost. The optimum soil pH figure is between 6.0 to 7.5.

Softwood or stem cuttings with a single leaf are taken for propagation. They will root in a propagating frame if kept at a temperature between 22 and 25 °C (71 to 77 °F) within four weeks.

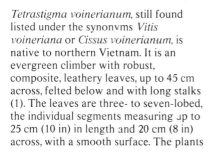

Tetrastigma voinerianum, still found listed under the synonvms *Vitis voineriana* or *Cissus voinerianum,* is native to northern Vietnam. It is an evergreen climber with robust, composite, leathery leaves, up to 45 cm across, felted below and with long stalks (1). The leaves are three- to seven-lobed, the individual segments measuring up to 25 cm (10 in) in length and 20 cm (8 in) across, with a smooth surface. The plants develop countless long, very elastic tendrils (2) twining in spirals around the support. Umbels of tiny and not very interesting flowers which open in early summer grow from the leaf axils. Since older specimens often become bare in their lower regions, new plants should be grown in time to replace them.

1

Black-eyed Clock Vine, Black-eyed Susan
Thunbergia alata

The genus *Thunbergia* covers some 100 species found in the wild in tropical Africa, Malagasy and in warm regions of Asia. They are woody species or herbs of chiefly climbing habit.

Thunbergia alata is the most common. It is a perennial from the coastal regions of south-eastern Africa and is grown in Europe as an undemanding house plant in cool rooms. It can also be grown in the garden as a climbing annual but has to be sown in early spring under glass.

As a potted plant it is stored in a place with a temperature of about 6 °C (43 °F) in the winter months. It is then cut back hard in early spring and left to shoot at a temperature od 15 to 18 °C (59 to 64 °F). It is regularly watered in the growing and flowering season, and given a liquid feed once every fortnight.

In the garden, *Thunbergia* needs a sunny, warm site, sheltered from the wind. The soil should be light, slightly alkaline and rich in nutrients. The plants need a support for climbing from the very beginning.

Fresh seeds are sown in March in trays of seed compost and then placed under glass. The seedlings germinate at a temperature of between 18 to 20 °C (64 to 68 °F) within 14 to 20 days. They are pricked out into small pots as soon as the seedlings can be handled and later potted on again if necessary. The young plants are set outside when no longer threatened by late frosts after a period of hardening off.

Thunbergia alata attains a height of 1.5 m (5 ft) in a favourable spot in the house or garden. The leaves are more or less heart-shaped, up to 8 cm (3 in) long. The flowers grow from leaf axils on long stalks, the flower tube being about 30 cm (12 in) long and terminated by five horizontally spreading lobes. The throat is black-brown. Outdoors, plants usually flower from mid-June until the first autumn frosts, when kept indoors they bloom for a longer period. Besides the species with a pale yellow flower and inside tube (1), there are also varieties in shades ranging from white to orange. *T. alata* var. *aurantiaca* has large orange flowers (2), var. *albiflora* is white with a black spot, 'Bakeri' has pure white, eyeless flowers and var. *lutea* produces yellow flowers without the dark spot. Specimens grown in pots need a support for climbing (3).

1

2

Wandering Jew
Tradescantia albiflora

Commelinaceae

Some 40 species of the genus *Tradescantia* are found in the wild in tropical South America. They are perennials mostly of trailing or pendent habit. The inconspicuous flowers appear usually in spring.

These undemanding and adaptable plants can be grown at temperatures between 5 to 25 °C (41 to 77 °F). They are tolerant of the dry air of modern homes. They do best in diffused light or semi-shade. The variegated forms need a lighter and warmer site than those with plain green leaves. Poor soil or shortage of nutrients bring out the colours in the foliage.

Watering must be adapted according to temperature and light. The variegated cultivars tend to revert to green foliage; so remove the green-leaved shoots as they appear and do not use them for cutting. The lower parts of older specimens become bare, and it is best to grow new plants every year.

Tradescantia albiflora, also known as *T. viridis,* is native to South America and was introduced to the southern regions of the United States. It can be grown from spring to autumn in window and balcony boxes, in pots, or in flower beds in the company of annuals.

Tradescantia fluminensis also comes from tropical South America. It differs from the previous species by having reddish stems and smaller leaves flushed violet below.

Tradescantia albiflora has fleshy, trailing stems, 30 to 50 cm (12 to 30 in) long, and sessile leaves measuring 6 cm (2 ¼ in) in length and 2.5 cm (1 in) across (1). Cultivars are also available, the most common one being *T. a.* 'Albovittata' with white-striped leaves (2). The variegated cultivars require more light and warmth than the species, otherwise their leaves change to green. If treated well in a suitable environment, the plants produce small whitish blossoms (3). These are short-lived, usually fading within a day, but since every inflorescence contains several dozen minute flowers, the plants may continue to bloom for weeks.

Wandering Sailor
Tradescantia blossfeldiana Commelinaceae

Tradescantia blossfeldiana is native to Argentina. It is an undemanding species suitable for less experienced amateur growers. It can be widely used indoors, placed in various containers or as ground cover in a large plant arrangement.

Tradescantia venezuelanica comes from Venezuela, as its specific name implies. It is used in hanging and wall containers where its elegant growth is best displayed.

Propagation is easy even for beginners. Tradescantias can be increased in any season from tip and stem cuttings. The cuttings should be 10 cm (4 in) long, stripped of the lowest leaves. Several cuttings can be inserted around the edge of pots filled with a peat-based compost. They will root within two weeks without cover. When rooted, they should be pinched a few times to promote bushy growth.

All species of *Tradescantia* are easy to grow and can be grown hydroponically. They can also be put in small wall containers with plain water. They make a good ground cover in large indoor plant arrangements. They can be grown in window and balcony boxes, or other containers, from May to October. They must be transferred inside by the end of September because they do not tolerate frost.

Tradescantia blossfeldiana (1) has thick, very hairy stems up to 30 cm (12 in) long. They grow erect at first but tend to droop with age. The leaves are 10 cm (4 in) long, red-violet below. The flowers are white-pink and appear from March to August.

Tradescantia venezuelanica has drooping stems and fine, glass-like leaves, smaller than *T. albiflora.* It forms a thick, trailing and much-branched growth (2).

The inflorescence is a raceme. The flowers (3) are composed of three green sepals and three fine, short-lived petals. There are six stamens around the pistil, with filaments covered by long hairs. The ovary has three compartments (triloculate) and matures into a capsule. There are two seeds in each compartment.

1

3

Nasturtium
Tropaeolum hybrids
Tropaeolaceae

Some 80 members of the genus *Tropaeolum* grow in the wild in mountainous regions of South America. They have fleshy, usually much-branched stems, either creeping or climbing.

Tropaeolum majus is native to Colombia, Ecuador and Peru. It grows as a perennial in the area of original distribution, but it is an annual under European conditions. It bears flowers from June to October depending on the time of sowing. The species does not exist in cultivation as it has been replaced by the large-flowered hybrids; cultivars with stems up to 2.5 m (8 ft) long and flowers about 7 cm (2 ¾ in) across.

Nasturtiums do well in any garden soil provided it is well-drained and not too rich in nitrogen. It flowers best in full sun as shade and moist soil promote the growth of leaves to the detriment of flowers.

Nasturtiums can be sown directly in their growing positions during April and early May. Seeds remain viable for two to four years. The seeds can also be sown in April in 8-cm (3-in) pots placed in a frame or greenhouse. Seedlings should be set out in their flowering positions in May; they will flower earlier than direct-sown plants.

Nasturtium is best displayed clambering over wire netting, wooden fences or as a trailing annual covering the ground or a bare slope.

Tropaeolum hybrids (1) are some of the least demanding and vigorously growing annuals. Their long stems are covered with a multitude of helmet-shaped flowers throughout the summer. A number of cultivars in many shades have been obtained. The stems, leaves and flowers are edible. Nasturtiums can be used as trailing subjects for hanging baskets and balcony boxes. As cut flowers they will last for up to 10 days in the vase and all the buds will open. Dwarf and non-trailing forms are also availabe. These are ideal for growing in pots and along the edges of borders.

Tropaeolum peregrinum, the Canary Creeper, from Peru reaches a height of

5 m (16 ft) in its native land. The leaves
have five to seven lobes and measure
about 13 cm (5 in) across (3). The flowers
are symmetrical, lemon-yellow, with
fringed petals (2). They are pleasantly
fragrant. The flowering season in Britain
lasts from July to October and, although
perennial in its native land, is grown as an
annual over here.

3

1

Greater Periwinkle
Vinca major

Apocynaceae

The genus *Vinca* includes only about five species found in the wild throughout Europe, Asia Minor and northern Africa. They are creeping sub-shrubs with ascending flower shoots. The leaves are evergreen, leathery and of varying shapes.

Vinca major frequents moist soils in the semi-shade of light woodland in southern Europe and Asia Minor. It can be grown as an indoor pot plant preferring cool situations and semi-shade. More usually it is grown in a sunny or shaded place in the garden, in window or balcony boxes.

When grown in a pot or box, it needs regular watering, and it should be fed occasionally in spring and summer. It needs plenty of light and cool temperatures in winter, and watering should be reduced. Repotting is done once every two or three years in a rich soil-based potting compost.

Periwinkle is usually propagated by cuttings taken in autumn or early spring. Several cuttings are put in pots placed in a frame or unheated greenhouse for the winter. Older plants can be increased by division of thick clumps. Care must be taken not to damage too many shoots and roots.

2

Vinca major (1) forms two types of shoots. The non-flowering runners that rapidly become woody are trailing and up to 80 cm (32 in) long. The flowering shoots are erect, growing to a maximum height of 30 cm (12 in). The leaves are up to 7 cm (2 ¾ in) long, the flowers are 4 cm (1 ½ in) across (2). Periwinkle blooms in spring and early summer, but individual flowers may also appear later if conditions are favourable. It is an excellent ground-cover plant, good for growing on a slope or bank or in the shaded area below taller-growing shrubs. Equally as vigorous as the species is the variegated cultivar, *V. m.* 'Variegata', with spotted, white-edged leaves (3).

Vinca minor comes from central Europe. Its non-flowering creeping stems produce roots, the flowering stems are only 15 cm (6 in) tall and bear flowers some three weeks earlier than *V. major.*

Chinese Wisteria
Wisteria sinensis

Leguminosae

The genus *Wisteria* comprises only 7 species. Their homeland is North America, China and Japan. They are climbing woody species with relatively tough stems and their deciduous leaves are yellow in autumn. The flowers hang in racemes and appear in spring but a second flowering may occur in late summer.

Wisteria sinensis, also referred to as *W. chinensis,* is the most common species. It was brought to Europe from China in 1816, where it had been grown as a garden plant for several centuries. It is the largest climber grown in Europe. It is quite hardy throughout the country. It can flower twice under favourable climatic conditions, which means that new racemes appear in the second half of summer. The second flowering, however, is far less profuse than the first.

Wisteria floribunda, the Japanese Wisteria is, as its name suggests, a Japanese species. It is only 8 m (26 ft) high, twines in an anti-clockwise direction and the violet inflorescences are up to 60 cm (24 in) long. It bears flowers in May and June.

Wisterias require a warm, sunny and sheltered site with deep, rich, well-drained soil. The plants are set out in spring, preferably against a house wall with a southerly exposure.

Wisterias grown in the garden are propagated by layering. Horticulturists graft cultivars on seedlings or root cuttings of the Chinese Wisteria in winter and grow them under glass. The plants grown from seeds flower poorly and lose the qualities of the parent plant.

Wisteria sinensis attains a height of up to 20 m (65 ft) and twines in a clockwise direction. The pinnate leaves are composed of up to 13 leaflets, each 8 cm (3 in) long. The flowers, arranged in racemes up to 30 cm (12 in) long (1), emerge simultaneously with leaves in April and May. Individual flowers are about 2.5 cm (1 in) across and fragrant. *W. sinensis* 'Alba' has white blossoms. In time wisterias form a thick, often gnarled trunk (2) capable of crushing even a gutter pipe when twining around it. They need a strong supporting construction. They are good subjects for pergolas, railings or as cover for unsightly constructions. They should not be planted too close to a wall to allow some circulation of air, otherwise the leaves yellow and wither.

1

2

Zebrina pendula

The small genus *Zebrina* has only four species originating mainly in Mexico. They resemble tradescantias by habit and are related to them. The pink or white flowers usually appear in spring.

Zebrina pendula is an undemanding house plant of trailing habit, thriving in almost any environment. It can be planted in a hanging basket or other suitable container and suspended from a wall bracket or from the ceiling. It is also used in mixed plantings and in window boxes.

Zebrina purpusii is of a more vigorous and compact growth. It has purple-red leaves if grown in a light site and greenish foliage if kept in the shade. It originates in Mexico. *Z. purpusii* 'Minor' has smaller, brown-flushed leaves.

Zebrina flocculosa is a rarely grown species deserving wider popularity.

All zebrinas have the same requirements for cultivation as tradescantias, only the winter temperatures must never drop below 12 °C (53 °F). The variegated cultivars need more light, otherwise their leaves turn green. They are tolerant of dry air in interiors. They should not be given any fertilizer as feeding destroys the attractive coloration of the foliage.

Zebrinas are easily propagated from tip or stem cuttings with several leaves. Several cuttings are placed in a pot filled with medium-heavy soil.

Zebrina pendula (1), often referred to as *Tradescantia zebrina*, is a trailing herbaceous plant from Mexico. The stems are about 40 cm (16 in) long and carry numerous leaves up to 6 cm (2 ¼ in) long. *Z. pendula* 'Quadricolor' is a slow-growing cultivar with white and pink stripes differing in width on leaves. *Z. flocculosa* is native to Central America. Its intensely blue flowers (2) appear in April.

Plectranthus parviflorus (3), still widely known as *P. australis,* is an evergreen perennial native to Australia and the Pacific islands. It needs a winter temperature of 8 to 10 °C (46 to 50 °F) and reduced watering. It can be kept outdoors in the summer.

P. oertendahlii (4) is a South African evergreen perennial of trailing habit, more demanding as to temperature and winter cultivation than the previous species. Cultivation of *Plectranthus* species is similar to *Zebrina.*

207

CARE OF CLIMBING PLANTS

If outdoor and house plants are to give pleasure, they have to be given regular care in order to keep them healthy and attractive.

Watering

The degree of water absorption depends on the size, age and stage of development of the plant, on the time of day, season, weather, light, temperature and atmospheric humidity, and also on the species.

Large-sized plants in full leaf transpire a far greater quantity of water than small plants, and consequently consume more moisture from the soil. In the winter months, during the period of relative rest, transpiration decreases and water consumption is lower. If a plant suffers from lack of water, its cellular tension drops, the stems droop, the leaves start to wither and the plant often perishes. On the other hand, persistent overwatering is equally dangerous because the roots cannot breathe. When house plants are overwatered, the soil in the pot becomes waterlogged, the drainage hole can get blocked and the compost turns sour. House plants should be watered daily in summer when it is very hot and the air is dry, but during the winter only once a week or even once a fortnight. Watering in the garden depends on the weather.

It is recommended to water early in the morning, because the plants take up water mainly during the day. The water should never be cold, but of room temperature. Tap water usually contains varying amount of chlorine or lime to which some plants are averse. Rain water is better, although it is often polluted.

Feeding

Plants need a certain amount of nutrients for healthy growth and development. They receive them chiefly in the form of weak solutions through the roots. Nutrient requirements are dependent on the species, the age of the plant, and on the season.

Basic feeding consists of adding fertilizers to the soil before planting or using a potting compost which contains fertilizers for repotting. These nutrients last from three to six months, but extra feeding will be necessary later.

Only healthy, well-rooted plants in full growth should be given fertilizers. The root system is disturbed by repotting, and until new roots have formed in the fresh soil, feeding is unnecessary and often harmful.

Plants should be fed mainly during the growing and flowering period. At the time of slow growth or rest, usually in winter, the water consumption is reduced and the roots could get burned if fertilizer was applied. Feeding usually begins in March or April and ends in September. Continued feeding promotes further growth and new shoots mature poorly. In the growing season when green parts are formed, plants need nitrogen in the first place. In the budding and fruiting periods, potassium and phosphorus are the most important elements.

House plants are usually fed once in a fortnight. The most convenient method is to apply a liquid fertilizer made up according to the instructions on the bottle or packet. Plants should be watered before feeding to ensure the compost is damp and to prevent damage to the roots. Outdoor climbing plants are top dressed with well-rotted compost in early spring; some species, such as honeysuckles, can be given a liquid feed a few times during the summer. Outdoor climbers are generally not particular over soil conditions and cultivation.

Repotting

Outdoor woody species should not be transplanted without good reason. Some species, such as clematis, do not tolerate transplanting.

Climbing and trailing house plants, especially young specimens, require regular repotting because they soon exhaust all available nutrients, the roots become pot bound in too small a pot and flowering and growth stop. The need to repot can be checked by turning a pot upside-down, knocking it lightly by the edge of a table, loosening the soil ball and lifting the pot with the other hand. If the roots fill the whole pot, the plant needs repotting.

The best time for repotting is early in spring or just before the onset of new growth. At that time the plant is in the best condition to cope with this disruption. Younger and rampant-growing potted plants need annual change of soil, older and slow-growing specimens can be transplanted once in two or three years. Frequently transplanted plants are potted up in a basic soil- or peat-based potting compost. Older plants prefer a richer soil-based potting compost that contains larger amounts of slowly released nutrients.

The size of the pot should be in proportion to the size of the plant and its roots. In a pot which is too large the roots take a long time to grow through all the soil, and the inactive soil becomes sour. A healthy and well-rooted plant needs a pot 2.5 cm (1 in) wider in diameter than the one it was formerly growing in. If the new pot is made of clay it should be stood in a pail of water for a few hours to soak. The compost in plastic, non-porous pots dries out less quickly than in clay containers.

Drainage of surplus water is important. The drainage hole at the bottom of the pot should be covered with a broken crock or some stone chips; during repotting the soil ball can be pushed out through this hole with a stick. For plants that need good drainage, a layer of broken crocks, quartz pebbles, fine gravel or coarse sand can be made at the bottom of the pot.

The plant can be removed from the pot more easily if watered a few hours before repotting. The root ball can be eased out by running a long, narrow-bladed knife between the compost and the wall of the pot. This procedure is used mainly for plants in terracotta pots which have not been transplanted for a long time.

The drainage layer is lightly covered with compost. The plant is placed in an erect position in the middle of the pot, held with one hand, while more compost is added with the other hand. The pot is shaken to ensure no air pockets are left, and the compost is pressed down with the thumbs around the edge. More compost is added to reach to about 2 cm (3/4 in) below the rim and allow some space for watering. A repotted plant should be positioned in the pot so the compost level remains the same as before. Climbing plants need a stick placed in the pot at the same time as the plant. The plant is then tied to the support in a way that does not hinder the formation of new stems or leaves.

A repotted plant should stand for a while in a shady place with slightly higher temperature and humidity than normal. Draught must be avoided. Watering is increased gradually according to the development of roots.

Shading

Even the most light-loving species must not be exposed to direct sunlight after repotting. In the first few weeks after repotting or planting out, outdoor or indoor climbing plants benefit from the shelter offered by a light wood, cotton or nylon mesh screen to prevent the root ball from drying out if the plant would otherwise be subjected to direct sunlight.

Most indoor climbers are intolerant of intense sunlight in the summer months, particularly those which in the wild inhabit the lower levels of a rain-forest. Shading can be desirable in spring or late winter when the sun suddenly appears in a cloudless sky and the weakened plants are not used to it. Overexposure causes fading of foliage, brown spots on the leaves or burnt foliage.

Venetian blinds are useful in south-facing windows: they can be rolled down or set in various positions, regulating the penetration of sunlight. Shading can be controlled automatically by a photoelectric cell in the greenhouse.

Pruning and shaping

Only plants capable of sprouting from dormant buds in lower parts of the stem tolerate hard cutting back. The tips of young plants are pinched out to induce branching. Older specimens are pruned to improve their shape. Drastic cutting back is necessary in woody species which tend to become bare in their lower regions; by cutting them back just above buds lower down the stems, they are forced to branch out.

In late-flowering species the cutting is done before the onset of new growth, while early flowering species are cut back immediately after blooming. Most indoor climbers are pruned between March and May.

Branches are cut as close as possible to leaf buds to avoid unsightly stumps. A sharp knife or pair of secateurs is used to make a smooth cut that heals quickly.

Weed control and soil aeration

Weeds compete with cultivated plants by depriving them of nutrients and moisture. Therefore they have to be cleared regularly. Gardening is easier and more successful if the soil is kept weed-free.

By aerating the soil, the soil crust is removed and air can reach the roots. In pots the surface of the compost is loosened with a pointed stick or similar tool, the garden soil is treated in usual ways, with a hoe or hand fork. Care must be taken not to damage the roots.

PROPAGATION OF CLIMBING PLANTS

Although propagation of ornamental plants is generally done by growers, an amateur gardener should be familiar with the basic principles, to be able to propagate his plants for his own pleasure or to give them to friends. The propagating methods of climbing plants are as many as there are uses of this group which boasts such a great variety of species. This section describes the most common methods.

Some annuals are easily propagated — they can be sown directly in their permanent site (e. g. Sweet Peas, ornamental beans and nasturtiums). The soil is prepared beforehand and the seeds sown in time so that they can germinate in late spring when there is little danger of them being damaged by frost. For best results the seeds must be fresh.

Half-hardy annuals, e.g. cobaea, gourd, eccremocarpus, hop, petunia and thunbergia, are sown in pots or seed trays and put in a greenhouse, frame or somewhere indoors. Later they are pricked out in small pots and then planted out when the last frosts are over after they have been hardened off.

Only species house plants are raised from seed (e.g. sedum, stephanotis, passion flower, plumbago); cultivars, if they produce seed, do not come true and the results can be disappointing. The seeds of some species soon lose their viability and should therefore be sown immediately after harvesting. They are sown in a proprietary seed compost, as evenly as possible and not too close. The seeds are covered with a layer of compost one to three times their own thickness, and a gap of 1 cm ($\frac{1}{2}$ in) below the rim of the container is left for watering. The seeds are kept in a warm place, in moist compost and covered with a sheet of glass and some paper. The seedlings germinate within a few days or weeks according to species; then the glass and paper must be removed immediately. Young seedlings must be shaded from scorching sunlight. They are pricked out into bowls, boxes or small pots as soon as they are large enough to handle, and potted on as necessary.

Seeds of tender species of woody plants, e.g. those of the genera *Akebia, Actinidia, Aristolochia, Campsis, Celastrus, Clematis, Lonicera, Rubus* and *Wisteria* are sown in a sandy compost in a seed tray or pot, and left in a shady place in the garden until the first frosts. They are then moved to a garden frame or greenhouse and the seeds germinate. Hardier species of these genera are sown directly in outdoor beds. The seeds of some species are stratified before sowing to speed up germination (e.g. woody species of the genera *Actinidia, Celastrus* and *Lonicera*). Stratification means mixing the seeds with sand and peat and placing the container in a moist and cool place in the garden until the time of sowing. There they are subjected to cold spells which are necessary before germination can take place.

Some species of climbing and trailing plants either do not yield viable seeds at all, or very rarely. These must be increased vegetatively. Some parts of the plant are capable of forming roots and shoots, and thus a new plant, when separated from the parent plant. These new plants grow much faster than those raised from seed. The plants propagated by vegetative means retain all the characteristics of the parent plant. The simplest way is division of clumps during repotting. Each section must have a good root formation.

Some plants (e.g. episcia and *Saxifraga stolonifera*) produce small baby plants at the tips of their stolons (shoots). As soon as the baby plants put out their own roots, they can be separated and planted in small pots. Bulbous and tuberous plants produce a certain number of small bulbs, tubers or rhizomes which can be separated during transplanting (e.g. gloriosa).

Akebias, trumpet creepers, brambles and other outdoor species grow suckers that can be separated and transplanted. The most common way of propagation is, however, by cuttings: a part of the stem, leaf or root is separated from the parent plant, inserted in moist compost where it sends out roots under favourable conditions and forms a new plant. Softwood cuttings are taken mainly from non-flowering new lateral growth of young specimens. The best time is spring, but the species that root readily can be increased in any season. The cuttings should be 4 to 7 cm (1½ to 2¾ in) long, or longer in some species. In the past it was recommended to take cuttings with a sharp knife to make a smooth cut, but greenwood cuttings of many species can be simply broken off just below a node, or snipped off with secateurs. The cuttings will root only in a warm, moist and shady place, such as a propagating frame. To maintain a high atmospheric humidity, the propagator is kept covered. Propagating frames can be thermostatically controlled and have their own built-in electric heat-

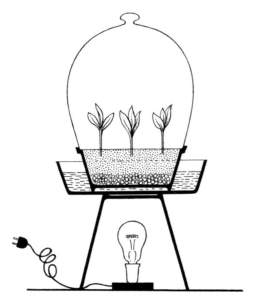

Pot propagator

ing system. Some species root easily and their cuttings can be put directly in pots of compost without any glass or polythene cover; they merely need to be placed away from direct sunshine, e.g. ivy or pelargoniums. There are plants that will root in a glass of water: e.g. allamanda, philodendron, scindapsus, tradescantia, zebrina and others. The cut surface should be submerged some 4 cm (1½ in) deep. When some long roots have formed, the cuttings can be potted up.

Hormone rooting powder can be applied to improve the rooting of some more difficult species. Sand, peat or a mixture of the two can be used as propagating compost, and coarse pearlite also gives good results.

House plants with woody stems (e.g. ficus, philodendron) can be air layered if they have lost their lower leaves or the plant has outgrown its position. A leaf is removed in the place where rooting is desired and an oblique cut is made about halfway through the stem. A matchstick or small pebble is inserted in the cut to keep it from closing up healing. The stem is wrapped in moistened peat moss kept in place with a piece of plastic-covered wire. To keep it moist, the moss is enveloped in polythene and tied at the top and bottom, above and below the cut. The best time for this type of propagation is June and July. The top is cut off after sending out enough roots which can be seen through the polythene, and it can be potted up; it is unnecessary to remove the peat moss coating.

Stem cuttings can be taken from some house plants (e.g. species of the genera *Monstera* and *Philodendron*). The trunk is cut into as many sections as there are buds, the cutting surfaces are sprinkled with charcoal to stop any oozing and the pieces are laid horizontally in propagating compost; roots will form and new plants will develop.

Root cuttings are used in species which bear buds on their roots, e.g. in members of the genera *Akebia, Campsis, Celastrus* and *Wisteria*. Each cutting should be 4 to 8 cm (1½ to 3 in) long and 1 to 2.5 cm (½ to 1 in) across. The cuttings are taken carefully late in autumn, and stored in moist sand in a frostproof place during the winter. They are moved into small pots of light soil-based potting compost in March and kept in a place with temperature of at least 9 °C (48 °C). They can be set outside in spring.

Hardwood cuttings are used for some outdoor climbers (e.g. members of the genera *Actinidia, Jasminum, Lonicera, Parthenocissus, Polygonum* and *Wisteria*). One-year-old ripened shoots are taken in autumn before the onset of heavy frosts, shortened to about 15 cm (6 in), tied in bundles and labelled, and stored in slightly damp sand or peat in a place where temperature does not exceed 3 °C (37 °F). In early spring the cuttings are planted out in an upright position in

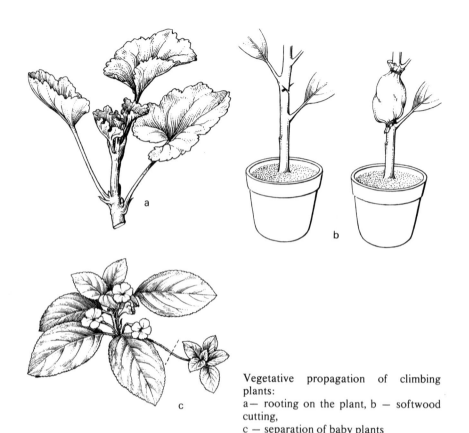

Vegetative propagation of climbing plants:
a— rooting on the plant, b — softwood cutting,
c — separation of baby plants

a well-prepared nursery bed outdoors so that the top bud is just above the soil level. The soil is covered with a mulch of peat or similar material to reduce evaporation and prevent the formation of a soil crust. The new plants are transferred to their permanent quarters either in autumn or the following spring; slow-growing species are left in the nursery bed for one to three years while they become established.

Almost all outdoor climbing and trailing plants can be increased by layering. One- or two-year shoots are bent down to the ground and covered with soil in several places. The underground parts of the stem will put out roots and the parts in the open will sprout new shoots. An incision is made at the rooting spot, a thin sliver is cut out and the cut surface is dusted with hormone rooting powder. After a year, two or more years later in some species, the rooted parts are cut free form the parent plant, lifted and transplanted to their permanent site.

In some cases climbing plants can also be propagated by indirect vegetative methods, such as grafting or budding.

TEN TIPS TO KEEP YOUR PLANTS HEALTHY

However much care is taken, it is sometimes impossible to avoid pests or diseases from occurring on plants in the garden or in the home. Regular inspection of the plants can, however, prevent many diseases getting established or a build-up of pests. Maintaining the good condition of climbing plants growing indoors or outdoors can be summarized as follows:

1. Observe the basic rules of hygiene and cultivation. The most important of these is to keep the plant clean; this involves keeping it weed-free, removing all withering flowers, using fresh compost when repotting, selecting healthy material in full growth for propagation, promptly removing diseased or damaged plants to prevent the trouble spreading and taking appropriate action at the first sign of any pest or disease.

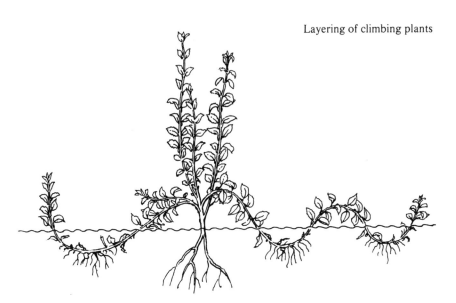

Layering of climbing plants

2. Respect the requirements of individual species as regards moisture. Many physiological troubles are caused by incorrect watering. Insufficient watering causes wilting, yellowing and drying out of leaves, leaf drop or shedding of buds and flowers. Persistent waterlogging, particularly when accompanied by low winter temperatures, brings about dropping, yellowing and rotting of the leaves and eventual death of the whole plant. Outdoor plants need a good supply of water in the soil which is usually taken care of by the natural rainfall.

3. Different species require different temperature regimes depending on the season and stage of development. Lack of warmth causes decrease or interruption of growth, damage to the root system and rotting of top growth and underground parts. The tissue of tropical climbers can be damaged by a sudden drop in temperature to 8 °C (46 °F). Conversely, positioning plants in an overheated environment will cause growth to become too lush and poor flowering; plants become more susceptible to diseases and attacks by pests.

A number of house plants require lower winter temperatures. It is preferable to choose a position where temperature can be controlled by regulating the source of heat rather than moving the plants around too much.

Tender outdoor climbers need a good protective covering of bracken or leaves in the winter months to protect them from frost, or — if they are particularly delicate — they should be moved to a greenhouse or stood indoors in a frostproof place.

4. Plants have varying light requirements which have to be considered: accordingly they are placed in the sun, semi-shade or shade. Shortage of light causes weak, etiolated growth, i.e. leaves are pale and small stems become weak and spindly. On the other hand, direct sunlight can burn the leaves and young shoots of plants which prefer shade or semi-shade. Plants do not tolerate too much moving around and tend to shed their buds or flowers if this happens.

5. Most climbing and trailing plants need airy conditions but do not tolerate draughts. Rooms have to be aired even in winter on frostfree days at midday. If your home is heated by gas or, more especially, a paraffin heater is used, only the toughest species will survive; delicate plants will wither, drop flowers and leaves, and gradually die. Outdoor plants can also be harmed by an atmosphere heavily polluted by industrial fumes. Fungus diseases spread quickly in lush growth where air circulation is poor.

6. Plants should be fed at the correct time and in the right concentration with respect to season and stage of development. Shortage of nutrients causes stunted growth or dropping of leaves and flowers. Overfeeding causes growth to become too luxuriant. A balanced feed is best; one with a high percentage of nitrogen and too little potassium and phosphorus encourages leafy growth and the plants consequently fail to produce flower buds. Shortage of a specific element (usually iron) and surplus of another (e.g. calcium) can cause chlorosis.

7. Virus diseases can be recognized by discoloration of foliage, deformation of leaves and flowers, stunted growth and even dying of the plant. They can be carried from contaminated plants to healthy ones by sucking insects (e.g. aphids), which have to be eliminated. The plants affected by viruses must be removed and burnt.

8. It is also vital to identify in time various bacterial diseases causing decomposition of soft tissues in underground parts and top growth. The diseased plants turn brown, grow tumors and perish. Bactericide sprays can be applied preventively.

9. Early elimination of fungus diseases and their carriers is also of great importance. The most common fungi are the powdery mildews (Erysiphaceae), forming whitish coating on foliage and young shoots; grey mould (Botrytis), covering leaves, buds and stems; rusts (Uredinales), causing rust-brown spots on the undersides of leaves; sooty mould (Caprodium), settling on the honeydew excreted by aphids and other pests. Treatment consists of spraying with an appropriate fungicide on outdoor plants; for indoor plants disease usually denotes poor growing conditions, so these should be improved. Powdery mildew develops in humid conditions, so improve ventilation. Grey mould is caused by moisture on the foliage, so remove affected leaves and water the plant from below. Cure the aphid problem with a suitable aphicide and sooty moulds will not form.

10. Control pests such as aphids, whiteflies, red spider mites, thrips, scales, mealy bugs and other species of sucking insects. In the garden there are other pests damaging underground parts of plants, e.g. millipedes, isopods and larvae of click beetles. It is preferable to remove the pests by hand if there are only a few, particularly in house plants because the correct application of pesticides can be a problem if ventilation is poor or fish are kept. When using chemicals, always follow the instructions on the packet or container and check whether

the product is suitable for use indoors and for the purpose required. It is recommended to make inquiries about a suitable preparation in a nursery or garden shop, because manufacturers bring out new and increasingly effective pesticides all the time.

Pergola with climbing clematis

INDEX

Page numbers in *italics* refer to illustrations

221

222